APOSTLES OF
Sartre

APOSTLES OF Sartre

Existentialism in America, 1945–1963

ANN FULTON

NORTHWESTERN UNIVERSITY PRESS Evanston, Illinois

Northwestern University Press
Evanston, Illinois 60208-4210
Copyright © 1999 by Northwestern University Press.
Published 1999. All rights reserved.
Printed in the United States of America
ISBN 0-8101-1290-6
Library of Congress Cataloging-in-Publication Data
Fulton, Ann.
Apostles of Sartre : existentialism in America, 1945–
1963 / Ann Fulton.
p.   cm.
Includes bibliographical references and index.
ISBN 0-8101-1290-6 (hardcover : alk. paper)
1. Existentialism—United States—History—20th
century.   2. Sartre, Jean Paul, 1905–   —Influence.
3. Philosophy, American—20th century.   I. Title.
B944.E94F85   1999
142'.78'0973—dc21   99-18175
                                          CIP

The paper used in this publication meets the
minimum requirements of the American National
Standard for Information Sciences—Permanence
of Paper for Printed Library Materials,
ANSI Z39.48-1984.

CONTENTS

PREFACE

This study is both a history of early Sartreanism's encounter with American philosophy and an exploration in the sociology of knowledge. It traces the manner in which early Sartreanism contacted American philosophy and the response Sartreanism received within the discipline between 1945 and 1963. The purpose of this study is to explain the sources of the checkered response to early Sartreanism among American philosophers. Why did so many seem to reject Sartreanism out of hand? And why did Sartre's ideas eventually begin to attract some positive attention? Dynamism has characterized Sartreanism's course in the American philosophical community, and this thesis helps explain that energy.

I would like to acknowledge, above all, the scholarly guidance and encouragement of Paul Boyer at the University of Wisconsin–Madison. He has taught me to isolate the substantive and discard the unnecessary. I am also extremely grateful for the philosophical wisdom and knowledge that David Newhall at Portland State University has extended to me through the years. His assistance and kindness will never be forgotten. Hazel Barnes, Wilfrid Desan, Eugene Kaelin, and Maurice Natanson—Sartre scholars all—have provided strong encouragement and have taken a personal interest in this project. My biggest debt, of course, is to my husband, Robert Janik. His support has always been the key. I would also like to thank my daughters Françoise and Rosalind for the many hours they gave me to finish this work.

1

Importing a Philosophy

Philosophical ideas and enthusiasms rose like bubbles to the surface of a glass of champagne in the Parisian intellectual community following the liberation of Paris in August 1944. One of them was the early existentialist thought of Jean-Paul Sartre. Efforts to understand, incorporate, or discredit Sartre's ideas became an important goal for many French philosophers and intellectuals during the two-year period of heightened interest that followed the outburst of widespread discussion of Sartreanism in the autumn of 1945. And, as part of the growing wave of attention paid to all strains of existentialism, Sartreanism continued to be an important current in French philosophical thought in the two decades following World War II.

In America the same phenomenon did not repeat itself. A voguish interest in Sartreanism sprouted among intellectuals in general in 1945, but relatively few American philosophers grappled seriously with Sartre's concepts. Although Sartre did not amass as many supporters in the immediate postwar philosophical dialogue in America as he did in France, he certainly made vital and enduring contributions to American philosophy. Due to the constraints of time, this study focuses specifically on the reactions of academic philosophers in secular institutions, although Catholic philosophers in Catholic universities were sometimes very much interested in the existentialist movement as a whole.

The period under study began in 1945 when American philosophers first learned about Sartreanism, and it drew to a close in 1963 when Hazel Barnes translated *Search for a Method*, the English version of the introduction to *Critique de la raison dialectique, précédé par Questions de méthode (Search for a Method* [1963]).[1] These were the years in which many American philosophers first confronted "early Sartreanism"—an existentialist inquiry noted for its emphasis on radical individualism and contingency. This stage of "early Sartreanism" in the history of Sartrean thought reached its end in the 1960s when those who did not already know that Sartre had superseded previous formulations with an effort to merge existentialism and Marxism became aware of the attempted union through *Search for a Method.*

Early Sartreanism's most significant impact was to challenge American philosophers to undertake the arduous process of philosophical reevaluation. Sartreanism prodded them to assess their methodological and ethical stances from a different perspective. It prompted some philosophers to question the rationale of narrowly analytic systems that had few referents outside the academic community. Early Sartreanism helped redirect attention to the individual as the philosophical wellspring of meaning and value. It encouraged philosophers to continue inquiries into the intricate modes of human consciousness and to reevaluate the possibilities and limitations of individual freedom. Of particular importance were the ethical questions that Sartre raised regarding the relativity of moral choices; in essence Sartreanism was of a piece with other contemporary inquiries that denied ethical absolutes. Instead, decisions should respond sensitively to the particular situations from which they arose.

Sartreanism also encouraged American philosophers to continue a predilection for viewing experience as a touchstone for philosophical thought. In the United States this emphasis was sometimes reflected in the high value placed on the use of scientific method, but this certainly did not preclude the existence of a thriving metaphysical current in American philosophy at midcentury. Sartreanism reminded individuals of the metaphysical implications of a philosophy rooted in experience.

The French philosophy also highlighted the need for international dialogue among philosophers. Commentators rued the frequent inability of Anglo-American analytic thinkers and speculative philosophers on the Continent to communicate with each other. Heightening the desire for increased internationalism was the hope that more productive conversations between philosophers at opposite ends of the ideological spectrum might encourage global peace in a tumultuous age. Sartreanism also provided a limited amount of professional opportunity for philosophers on the margin, most notably women. The American philosophical community at midcentury was overwhelmingly male, one in which women often found it difficult to gain a toehold. As an incoming philosophy about which little was initially known, Sartreanism provided some female philosophers fluent in French and familiar with Continental thought a small window through which they could enter the profession.

Early Sartreanism's evolution in America from 1945 to 1963 constituted a legitimization process that did not culminate in full assimilation. One important channel through which that legitimization process flowed was William James's radical empiricism. Philosophers recognized significant parallels between Sartre's and James's thought: an empiricism broadly conceived; rejection of a block universe narrowly encased in an unyielding, rationalistic structure; and an intense interest in how individuals constructed their world through meaning and values. This awareness of parallels between Sartreanism and William James's strain of pragmatism—a philosophy long identified, rightly or wrongly, as somehow quintessentially American—spoke eloquently of Sartreanism's resonance with critical issues in mid–twentieth-century American philosophy.

In sum, Sartreanism helped revitalize American philosophy at a time when many philosophers were worried that their discipline had lost its reason for being; science seemed to have cheerfully assumed philosophy's former role as the fount of all wisdom. With its interdisciplinary blending of philosophy, literature, and psychology and with its focus on the human construction of meaning and contemporary social issues, Sartreanism helped invigorate philosophy by drawing into the edges of its fold a larger number of people. Sartreanism may not have won over many professional philosophers at midcentury, but it definitely brought more students to their office doors; the French philosophy was a very important instigator of the wave of interest in the broad movement of existentialism that began to sweep over college campuses by the middle of the 1960s.

Sartreanism also provided the ultimate service of challenging philosophical beliefs and methodologies, a function that served as the springboard to the formation of new constructs. David Newhall, a professor emeritus of philosophy at Portland State University in Oregon who specialized in ethics and the philosophy of history, remembered how excited he was when introduced to Sartreanism as a graduate student at Princeton University in 1947: "I listened eagerly to my colleagues as they laid out the basics of Sartre's thought as we drove back to Princeton after a night out. I had read about Sartre in the paper and I was anxious to know more, for he sounded so alive."[2]

* * *

A brief overview of the intellectual and personal sources of Sartre's thought deepens understanding of the evolutionary course of Sartreanism in American philosophy. The Sartrean concepts under consideration are those philosophical ideas Sartre developed prior to the decision to dissolve his existentialism into Marxism in the late 1950s. These ideas are most completely outlined in *Being and Nothingness: A Phenomenological Essay on Ontology* (1956), originally published in 1943 as *L'Être et le néant: Essai d'ontologie phénoménologique,* and in *Existentialism* (1947), originally published as *L'Existentialisme est un humanisme* in 1946.[3]

Sartre's unique brand of existentialism is best understood in relation to the many streams that comprise the wide river of ideas collectively labeled "existentialism." Existentialism is a philosophical school inasmuch as its members share particular themes but frequently disagree on specific concepts. Telling subjects include human consciousness and freedom, situational ethics, and energetic opposition to any philosophical system building. Negative human experiences often offer a springboard for philosophic reflection. Individuals in existentialist thought are beings harshly dropped into a problematic world where endless, difficult choices press upon them. The most critical aspects of existence cannot be universalized through reason, and reality reveals itself only in immediate, dramatic experience. Existentialists regard human consciousness as radically free but unable to give itself a definable essence.[4] Both atheism and theism crosscut the ideas of existentialist philosophers. Atheistic existentialists disagree on many issues but they do stress the harsh nature of individual existence, owing to the absence of God and human freedom to create an independent future. Theistic existentialists have their quarrels too but maintain the transcendence of spiritual being over existence.[5]

The roots of existentialism are firmly planted in the mid–nineteenth-century opposition to Hegelian idealism. These idealistic threads served as a negative source because idealism was the dominant viewpoint from which rebels fervently wished to escape. Søren Kierkegaard, Friedrich Nietzsche, and Karl Marx were largely responsible for providing the philosophical climate that would enable twentieth-century existentialism to bloom. The specific doctrines of these three men were not always closely followed, but their philosophical tonalities and lines of inquiry created a lush environment for growth.[6]

The opposition of the Danish philosopher Kierkegaard (1813–55) to Georg Hegel's totalizing system of absolute knowledge was the initial reflex that became the wellspring of modern existentialism. Kierkegaard violently rejected Hegelianism and committed himself to bringing the specificity of individual experience to the foreground.[7] By the mid–twentieth century, however, Hegelianism was reinterpreted and became the source of key concepts that existentialists incorporated. Kierkegaard's perspective included resistance to existing social and religious institutions. His mood was intense, highly interiorized, and negative, a frame of mind sometimes mirrored in later existentialist thought. Fundamental Kierkegaardian tenets included a belief in personal freedom and possibility.

The German philosopher Nietzsche (1844–1900) was also a vocal opponent of absolute idealism. He criticized Christianity for denigrating the importance of this world, reason, and human excellence. Nietzsche's dissatisfaction with social mores, his belief in creative activity, and support of individual freedom were ideas that echoed loudly in existentialist thought.[8] Marx (1818–83) also helped prepare the ground. Marx sounded a fundamental note that would long reverberate in existentialism when he argued that individuals were deeply affected by the nature of their work and that capitalism was a primary source of social alienation.[9] Existentialists would later build on both Marx's and Kierkegaard's fear that industrialization threatened the dignity of the individual, and they too stressed the importance of human values in an increasingly technical world.

* * *

Like many other existentialist philosophers, Sartre also drew on his interpretation of the circumstances of his own life when he developed his philosophy. Born on June 21, 1905, Sartre was left fatherless at the age of fifteen months. As a young child he basked in the undivided attention his mother showered upon him and later the drama of having no father appealed to his imagination: "The death of Jean-Baptiste was the big event of my life: It sent my mother back to her chains and gave me freedom."[10] The importance Sartre attached to individual liberty had deep roots in his perception of the license he experienced in childhood.

Charles Schweitzer, Sartre's grandfather, doted on him too, and this anti-Catholic patriarch left an indelible mark. The old man encouraged him to read voraciously; his grandfather proudly announced that Sartre's "kind of talent is characteristically verbal . . . he dreams of nothing but adventure and poetry."[11] An important vein in Sartre's early existentialism was his belief in the wisdom and propriety of utilizing his literary talent to explain his philosophy to the public. Schweitzer's unquestioning support of the moral code of the French bourgeoisie, however, had a negative impact. In reaction, Sartre later developed a hatred for any characteristic he associated with the middle class. This tendency was reinforced when his mother married the naval engineer Joseph Mancy. Sartre deeply resented the intrusion of Mancy, whom he caricatured as the "ultimate bourgeois," into his relationship with his mother.

At lycées in La Rochelle and Paris, Sartre was introduced to the philosophers typically included in beginning philosophy classes: René Descartes, Gottfried Leibniz, Baruch Spinoza, Immanuel Kant, and Henri Bergson. Sartre's interest in philosophy intensified when he read Bergson in preparation for the Sorbonne's prestigious teachers' college, the École Normale Supérieure. In Bergson he found the description of "what I believe to be my psychological life."[12] Sartre entered the École Normale in 1924 and prepared to teach philosophy. Here Simone de Beauvoir and Sartre began their early romance. Beauvoir's later memoir provides a picture of Sartre in these years; she recalled that Sartre and his "normalien friends" considered themselves "private anarchists."

They discussed politics, leaned toward socialism, and despised capitalism but were not truly politicized. Sartre was already at work on his concept of radical freedom.[13]

Two important breaks occurred between 1931 and 1944 when Sartre was immersed in teaching and writing. In 1933, the year Hitler came to power, Sartre traveled to the French Institute in Berlin to study the phenomenology of Edmund Husserl (1859–1938) in depth. Sartre was fascinated by Husserl's attempt to understand objects solely on the basis of their description rather than through an analysis of their meaning; Sartre rejected the "alimentary philosophies" of idealism and realism that viewed the mind as a spider "that drew things into its web, covered them with white spittle and slowly assimilated them, reducing them to its own substance."[14]

Sartre's teaching career was interrupted when he was drafted and assigned to a meteorological unit. Captured by the Germans on 20 June 1940, he was imprisoned for a year. Although he escaped in 1941, prison camp left an indelible mark because incarceration challenged Sartre's first philosophical formulations of freedom. He moved away from his emphasis on radical individual liberty toward a much stronger belief in the necessity of social and political freedom.

Throughout the late 1930s and 1940s, Sartre wrote voluminously. *L'Imagination* (*Imagination: A Psychological Critique* [1962]), Sartre's exploration of the imagination's function, was published in 1936. *La Nausée* (*Nausea* [1949]), a unique philosophical novel that included some of Sartre's early visions of freedom and contingency, appeared in 1938.[15] His philosophical studies revealed critical reflections on Husserlian phenomenology. Although outside the mainstream of Anglo-American interests, these studies captured the attention of a number of European philosophers who, like Sartre, wanted to understand reality through description rather than analysis.

Sartre valued Husserl's concept of intentionality and contingency, but he quarreled with other ideas. Unlike Husserl, Sartre believed that consciousness had no content and that ego was the intentional object of consciousness in the world. He established the prereflective cogito as the primary consciousness in *La Transcendance de l'ego: Esquisse d'une description phénoménologique* (1936) (*The Transcendence of the Ego: An Existentialist Theory of Consciousness* [1957]).[16] This work countered the traditional idea of identity by rejecting the primacy of the Cartesian ego and Husserl's transcendental ego; Sartre argued that the ego is not in consciousness but in the world and both ego and world are objects of consciousness.

Sartre was not pleased with the changes his publishers required for *L'Imagination,* so in 1940 he wrote *L'Imaginaire: Psychologie phénoménologique de l'imagination* (*The Psychology of the Imagination* [1948]). *L'Imaginaire* tackled the relationship of the imagination to the problems of freedom and contingency. In 1939 *Esquisse d'une théorie des émotions* (*The Emotions: Outline of a Theory* [1948]) was sandwiched between these books.[17] Together these three works represented Sartre's analysis of imagination and emotion as structures in intentional consciousness. Sartre completed *L'Être et le néant,* a massive work that provided a systematic explanation of his early philosophy, in 1943. In it he grappled with the question of how that which is given to consciousness could be rescued from subjectivity.

* * *

After World War II, Sartreanism became a philosophical fad in France, and Sartre's thought in the early postwar years continued to respond to the philosophical, political, and literary issues of the day. His writings revealed the intensification of his belief in the necessity of political and social commitment. This was expressed initially in *L'Existentialisme est un humanisme* in 1946 and reverberated in later novels and plays. Sartre's postwar perspectives were also voiced in *Les Temps Modernes,* a political and literary review that he helped found and that first appeared on 15 October 1945. The review provided Sartre with a ready forum for his opinions on the issues of the day.[18] At this point Sartre's political stance was one of independent, critical support of the French Communist Party. He believed that Marxism was the only viable political ideology for the future, but he strongly disagreed with Stalinized Marxism; Sartre sought a nondogmatic form.

Until the 1956 invasion of Hungary, Sartre reacted angrily to periodic attacks on him by Communist Party members who perceived Sartreanism as bourgeois idealism, but he did not condemn party actions. Instead he worked diligently to meld his existentialism with a "purified" Marxism. This distilled Marxism was the antimaterialistic, humanistic ideology that Sartre felt was outlined in Marx's early works.[19] Two milestones along Sartre's road to ideological reconciliation were his decision to embed individual freedom more deeply in historical context and his recognition of the social weight of class differences.

The Soviet invasion of Hungary in 1956 interrupted Sartre's limited acceptance of Communist Party ideology. He completely broke with Stalinism, and this period ushered in a reconciliation between Sartre and anti-Stalinist Marxists. As the Cold War thawed, these partisans of differing ideologies were a little more willing to contemplate a synthesis of existentialist and Marxist ideas.[20] Sartre also campaigned against French colonialism in Algeria in the 1950s. Serving as a sort of anti-ambassador, he lectured internationally to protest colonialism. These activities were rightly construed by some Americans as searing criticism of their own foreign policy.[21] Sartre's reflections on the feasibility of blending existentialism and Marxism emerged in *Critique de la raison dialectique* (*Critique of Dialectical Reason* [1976]).[22] It was the first segment of a reflection on the limits of dialectical reason that remained unfinished. Sartre analyzed Marxism as a synthetic form of thought and separated it from the practice of Stalinism; he hoped to establish the dialectical mode as a philosophical anthropology that would uncover the nature of the individual in the world.

* * *

The philosophical roots of Sartre's early existentialism extended back to the founding fathers—Kierkegaard, Nietzsche, and Marx—but Sartre was also deeply imprinted by the ideas of Descartes, Husserl, Heidegger, and Hegel. He was searching for a philosophy that would counteract absolute idealism and provide a materialistic viewpoint that confirmed individual freedom.[23] For Sartre, as for many others schooled in the French tradition, Cartesianism was a deeply embedded framework. Although Sartre rejected the idealistic strain in Cartesianism with a vengeance and pushed Descartes's ego out of consciousness, he had high praise for Descartes's "revolutionary" commitment to human subjectivity.[24]

Sartre's faith in reason was certainly not as substantial as Descartes's, but Sartre was far from embracing irrationalism. Sartre developed a "logic of the absurd" that rationally accounted for illogic. This culminated in the concept of a prereflective consciousness, one of whose functions was the ability to make irrational choices. Yet, for Sartre, the best choices remained the rational decisions of a reflective consciousness. Sartre derived from Cartesianism a view of human freedom as something the individual was necessarily aware of and of consciousness as directed toward an object. Here he found affirmation of creative freedom, but it was liberty that Sartre would increasingly see limited by historical situation.[25]

Still searching for a satisfactory means of escaping absolute idealism, Sartre discovered Husserlian phenomenology in the early 1930s. Husserl created a philosophical system in which the phenomenological method became an ontology; the phenomenon was not simply an appearance but a disclosure of being. The basis of Husserl's methodology was phenomenological reduction. The philosopher's field was reduced to primary experiences; phenomena were described as they appeared, and explanations were based solely on descriptions rather than on a priori theories.

Sartre agreed with the concept of reduction, but he vacillated between trying to make it a purer, more scientific analysis and using it as a layperson's tool to discover what hid behind the self.[26] He rejected Husserl's philosophy in its entirety because of its alignment with the German idealistic tradition. Husserl's ultimate goal was to reflect on the functions by which essences became conscious and the discovery of the nature of essences. These objectives were opposed to Sartre's concept of philosophizing as an inquiry grounded in human concreteness. Sartre concluded that Husserl had not stuck steadfastly to the phenomenological viewpoint as a basis for an ontology.

Sartre was also deeply indebted to the work of the German philosopher Martin Heidegger (1889–1976). Heidegger explored the negativities of the "not-yet" and the "no-longer," and Sartre followed by describing in greater detail others that defined the human condition. Sartre adopted Heidegger's view that the individual's past was not a compendium of completed events; the meaning of the past was continually reinterpreted to determine its relevance for future projects. Sartre also borrowed from Heidegger the idea of developing a special vocabulary to describe philosophical categories. The sometimes tongue-twisting new terminology was intended to define categories more accurately and to draw attention to the difference between what the new labels stood for and their more traditional analogues. Although both Heidegger and Sartre believed that being preceded essence, Heidegger also argued that being preceded existence. While Sartre's objective world was an instrumental hierarchy of things available to human possibilities, Heidegger's objects became important for their ability to speak for themselves regarding being.[27]

Sartre began reading Hegel in 1939 to deepen his understanding of

Marx and was immediately drawn to the Hegelian constructions of negativity and consciousness. His attraction was fueled by the Hegelian renaissance that blossomed in France in the 1940s. This renewed attention to Hegel was not a rejuvenated idealism but an interest in Hegel's emphasis on the historicity of reason and the rationality of history. Sartre, like many other French intellectuals after the war, was eager to rid himself of atemporal concepts.

A fundamental idea in *L'Être et le néant* was the adaptation of Hegel's view that the individual sought a reconciliation between desires for being and nothingness that culminated in absolute knowledge. Contrary to Hegel, Sartre argued that such a union was impossible. Sartre followed Hegel until the final synthesis that brought absolute knowledge, but for Sartre such a totality was only a hopeless wish that ontologically characterized human beings. Hegel worked toward an idealistic end, hoping to establish the supremacy of reason, while Sartre worked toward an existentialist end, hoping to verify the supremacy of human existence.[28]

After *L'Être et le néant* inspired a flood of Marxist criticism in the early 1940s, Sartre's central project was to reconcile Sartreanism and Marxism. He valued key ideas in Marx's early work, including a definition of freedom as a condition grounded in historical situation and the use of a dialectic in which facts were produced within the higher unity of a whole. But even when he reached the conclusion that existentialism should be dissolved into Marxism, Sartre envisioned his early principles as essential correctives for applied Marxism. He hoped to remind Marxists to recognize the impossibility of impartially analyzing the historical process and to reestablish the importance of individual freedom.[29]

* * *

The intricate interweaving of his own ideas with those of other philosophers that Sartre accomplished in his early works was not immediately well known, but the broad brushstrokes of early Sartreanism were avidly discussed by Parisian intellectuals after the liberation of France. Simone de Beauvoir called it the "existentialist offensive," a period of time from the autumn of 1945 through the spring of 1947 in which Sartreanism became a philosophical fad in France. Sartre and Beauvoir were celebrities, and photographers snapped their pictures greedily. Janet Flanner, the French correspondent for the *New Yorker,* told Americans in December 1945 in her "Paris Journal" column that

"Sartre is automatically fashionable now among those who once found Surrealism automatically fashionable."[30] The popularity of Sartreanism among cultural faddists, left-leaning intellectuals, Parisian youth, and even a few ex-Vichyites went hand in hand with virulent criticism. The majority of Communist Party members, Catholics, and right-leaning intellectuals harangued Sartre for advocating a philosophy that, in their view, further unraveled the country's moral fabric. This fear of moral dissolution formed the bedrock of opposition to Sartre.

Several factors created a milieu that nurtured the popularity of Sartreanism. The simultaneity of Sartre's and Beauvoir's literary efforts helped to spark the initial intense flurry of interest in 1945. *L'Être et le néant* now received the scrutiny it escaped in 1943.[31] Sartre's lecture, "L'Existentialisme est un humanisme," was delivered at the Club Maintenant in October, and it too attracted much attention. At this crowded talk, Sartre tried to simplify and to popularize the concepts he presented in *L'Être et le néant*. Sartreanism was also kept in public view by *Les Temps Modernes*. Left-leaning papers surfaced immediately after the liberation and Parisian intellectuals read them hungrily. The media-wise Sartre took advantage of the vacuum left by the suppression of collaborationist publications; Sartre helped found *Les Temps Modernes* so that he might present his ideas quickly and have them widely read.

Sartreanism's initial postliberation appeal was also a product of the mythology that quickly enveloped the French Resistance. Resistance participation was glorified by many intellectuals; freedom fighters were handily transformed into saviors who would salvage France's future. A certain nostalgia emerged for the occupation years, during which individuals had been able to demonstrate their political activism and moral commitment. Sartre received recognition in this climate of adulation and wistfulness because at that time some considered him a Resistance hero. Although he never engaged in physical confrontations with the Germans, he had expressed his sympathy with the movement in his writing, his membership in the National Writers' Committee, and his organization of a Resistance group. Particularly important was Sartre's emphasis on the difficulty of moral choice in life-and-death situations, a theme integral to Resistance activities.

The voguish interest in Sartreanism encouraged Sartre's acceptance of the label "existentialist." When Gabriel Marcel (1889–1973), a French philosopher who blended Catholicism with existentialist principles, first applied the term to Sartre at a colloquium in 1945, Sartre rejected the epithet and said that his was a philosophy of existence. Within a few months he reconsidered and adopted the label because he hoped it would help people grasp his ideas. Liberated Paris provided a conducive environment for a dynamic philosophy immersed in the political and social issues of the day. Shackled for four years by German and Vichyite doctrines, many were eager to listen to a philosophy that expressed qualified hope. Although some misunderstood Sartreanism as only a nervous pessimism, others recognized that it contained optimistic as well as anxious notes. Sartre believed that by insisting upon personal commitment and social responsibility, the French people might overcome the nation's challenges and create a luminous future. Sartreanism therefore resonated with both the dreams and despair of postliberation France.

The vogue of Sartre's ideas was also the product of nationalistic sentiments among members of the French press. This heightened nationalism was expressed in the glorification of all French cultural products to demonstrate France's invincible vitality. It was one way of denying the disturbing fear that France might never regain the international political and cultural prestige it had enjoyed before World War I.[32] Awareness of a loss of power, the slow erosion of the Cartesian classical tradition, and dissatisfaction with conservative bourgeois morality had surfaced in the 1920s and by the 1930s had become a matter of some concern. In the 1940s the necessity of retooling cultural, moral, and political traditions was a given for progressive-minded people.[33]

The popular French press gave Sartre a great deal of coverage for much less profound reasons. Sartreanism attracted young people who were photogenic and fond of indulging in exciting escapades as they roamed the glamorous new nightspots that sprang up after the liberation. The Parisian popular press found good copy in recounting the drinking, dancing, and discussion marathons that took place in the cellar jazz clubs and the cabarets of St.-Germain-des Prés. Sartre and his followers were the new "bad girls and boys." The attraction between Sartre and young Parisian writers and intellectuals was mutual. The youth were appreciative of the care with which he criticized their work and his attempts to show them their social and moral responsibility as elites. Jacques Guicharnaud, a member of the group of young people that formed around Sartre, recalled: "[Sartre] attached us to him by his patent kindness, by the clarity of his articulation, by his refusal of any polite compromise in argument, by the call that went out from him to what we really were."[34]

Some were simply fascinated by Sartreanism because it was new. Students whom the philosopher-poet Jean Wahl had never met before stopped him in the street, exclaiming, "Surely you are an existentialist!" Then they urged him to explain Sartre's ideas.[35] Sartre associated with young people because he appreciated their insouciance and interest in new concepts, but he was also paternalistic. He liked the idea that Sartreanism had changed their perception of the world. The appearance of philosophical, literary, and journalistic efforts by Sartre and a need for hope, nationalism, and sensationalism created a milieu that encouraged Sartre's popularity between 1945 and 1947.

* * *

Other nurturants were more overtly political. Sartre revealed the importance of the French desire for collective action when he described the atmosphere surrounding the Parisian routing of the Germans in August 1944: "It [the liberation] begins like a festival, and even today, the Boulevard Saint-Germain, deserted and swept intermittently by machine-gun fire, keeps its air of tragic solemnity. In this time of drunkenness and joy everybody feels the need to plunge back into the collective life."[36] The aura of a festival, the drunkenness used to celebrate and to dampen anxieties, were moods and states characteristic of the political climate. Exhilarating optimism and nervous apprehension about the future were in the air.

The time-honored goals of liberty, equality, and fraternity that the Resistance embraced and the restructuring of social institutions suddenly seemed attainable. Although not everyone supported these objectives, for several years after the war the French political mood favored change. Sartreanism's popularity was enhanced because it celebrated freedom and the possibility of reform. The thought of redesigning France's infrastructure naturally generated anxiety too, as did the problem of getting the nation back on its feet and of ensuring international peace. Beyond that were worries created by production and transportation shortages, unreturned prisoners, and an escalating cost of living. Sartreanism struck a sympathetic nerve because it acknowledged the arduousness of simple existence.

The politics of postliberation Paris was molded by an ethical search too. "[W]hat France needs most," observed Flanner, in her *New Yorker* column "Paris Journal" in December 1944, "is not the salvation offered by any political party but a revival of morality."[37] Sympathetic readers of Sartre realized his commitment to this difficult goal. The decline of international prestige, the 1940 fall, the indignities of the occupation, and the thriving postwar black market were viewed by many as sure signs of moral decay; political arguments revolved around how best to struggle out of France's "immoral morass." Sartre was appreciated because he tried to construct a political morality that embraced the enduring principles of liberty, equality, and fraternity.

War and prison camp affirmed the significance of solidarity and community for Sartre and challenged the morality of individual authenticity that appeared in *L'Être et le néant*. The ethical code in that work made personal integrity the touchstone. The goal was subjective authenticity, achieved by eliminating self-deceptions. Sartre's postwar search for a moral path was an accretion of the more narrowly individualistic morality of *L'Être et le néant* and that of a community-oriented ethics. "The individual without ceasing to be a monad," he observed, "becomes aware that he is playing in a more than individual game."[38] Personal authenticity was not discarded, but the route to that end was through collective effort to build a better future.

Sartreanism was also attractive to the noncommunist Left because it adhered to the political goals of the Resistance movement. Socialist political values were increasingly appealing to intellectuals and working-class people. The socialism they adopted, however, had no specific agenda, and their loyalty to it fluctuated.[39] Resistance political ideology reached its peak immediately following the liberation, but its real political power was already ebbing when Sartreanism became popular in the autumn of 1945. For the rest of the decade, however, Resistance dreams flourished in left-wing Parisian intellectual circles. Writers like Sartre who adhered to those ideals were lionized.

Sartreanism was greatly affected by the strength of the Communist Party during the peak of its appeal. Sartre's ideas of course were attacked by party members, but in the process they received greater publicity. The Communists occupied a privileged place in the political thought of uncommitted intellectuals on the Left such as Sartre. Unconvinced of the rectitude of party-driven Marxism, they did believe that it was the most promising corrective of bourgeois democracy. Unlike American intellectuals, they were not surrounded by a deep-seated national bias against communism.

The French philosophical community was vibrantly alive in the aftermath of the war; ideas about the individual, God, being, nothingness, and subjectivity were urgently explored by philosophers searching for relevance to the experience of war. Sartreanism was nourished by this quest. Above all, philosophers were hoping to find categories, principles, and modes of thought that would help them better understand the human condition within the historical context of postwar France. Sartre was one of those thinkers who described himself as a "hunter of meaning."[40]

An important ingredient in Sartreanism that elevated its significance was its acceptance of a relatively new French philosophical standard—the criterion of the concrete. Beginning in the late 1920s, many young French philosophers shunned idealism and turned toward systems grounded in the experience of the concrete—of existence. Sartre's acceptance of this criterion heightened the merit of his ideas because this standard was so widely accepted in the philosophical community. The French philosopher Jacques Havet stressed its impact in "French Philosophical Traditions between the Two Wars," an essay written for *Philosophic Thought in France and the United States,* a collection of essays published in 1950 to help clarify contemporary currents in Anglo-American and Continental philosophy: "The search for a concrete understanding of man . . . may portend more than a revolution in the concepts within philosophy; it may mean a completely new definition of philosophy itself."[41]

The standard of concreteness was a key ingredient in the early twentieth-century rebellion against academic idealism—the revolt initially described in France as a pursuit of philosophy grounded in experience when it surfaced in the 1920s: "[W]hat interested us . . . was real men with their labors and their troubles. . . . At that time one book enjoyed a great success . . . Jean Wahl's *Toward the Concrete* . . . it embarrassed idealism by discovering in the universe paradoxes, ambiguities, conflicts still unresolved."[42] This quest underwent a relabeling process and emerged as the search for existence in the 1940s. Major schools of thought such as Marxism and Thomism felt the impact of the movement when their spokespeople tried to incorporate such existentialist agendas as a focus on individual existence into their conceptual framework.

Increasing French interest in phenomenology throughout the 1930s and 1940s also helped to expand the appeal of existentialism because the two movements were commonly linked together. Sartre's early use of Husserlian phenomenology to explore existentialist themes in the 1930s played an important role in tightening the connection between phenomenology and existentialism. His decision to accept existentialism as a label after publishing *L'Être et le néant*, which had as its subtitle *"Essai d'ontologie phénoménologique,"* helped to wed phenomenology and existentialism in many philosophers' minds.[43] Sartreanism also played an integral role in the French philosophical dialogue because of its clear link to the Hegelian renaissance. This revival reached full strength after the war when Hegel's early works became readily available. Much of the interest in Hegel was an outgrowth of the appeal of Marxism; French intellectuals were drawn to Hegel as a primary source for Marx.[44]

The critical concept that emerged from this intersection of existentialism, the Hegelian revival, and Marxism was Hegel's vision of the rationality of history and the historicity of reason. Now history and reason were not antithetical; thinking individuals were placed inside historical reality and their ideas reflected historical forces. Advocates of this view argued that Hegel revealed that if reason were considered within a historical context, events that appeared irrational could be regarded as distortions retaining the possibility of future rationality. Concepts like these provided the French thinkers with a philosophical framework that would allow them to make sense of the horrors of World War II.

The interrelatedness of history and the individual was minimized in works Sartre published before the end of the war, but later this construct became a dominant theme. Sartre's continued attempt to define the relationship between individual action and historical forces naturally heightened the value of his philosophical contribution for those to whom this was a central concern. The humanistic reading of Marx popular with Sartre, Beauvoir, and other French intellectuals was helpful too because it contained ideas compatible with Sartreanism. Key principles in this Marxist revisionism were the concepts of "total man" and alienation. The idea of "total man" constituted a rejection of "*homo economicus*," the model of the individual inherent in economic determinism. "Total man" was contoured by economic forces but also by physiological, psychological, historical, social, and political ones.

Humanistic readings of early works by Marx also made economic alienation a product rather than a cause of Marx's fundamental construction of alienation. Human alienation was stressed, as a fundamental condition based on the failure to acknowledge personal humanity and to recognize the individual's potential to shape nature and society. Reinterpretations of Marx's model of the self and alienation gave currency to Sartreanism; Sartre, too, was trying to grasp the total person and to demonstrate that human freedom offered a means of controlling natural and social forces.[45]

The French philosophical milieu from which Sartreanism emerged in the mid-1940s had a great deal of surface variation, but significant lines of demarcation were few. Richard McKeon, a philosopher at the University of Chicago who studied at the Sorbonne and the École des Hautes Études in the 1920s and who was committed to increasing internationalism in philosophical dialogue, described the postwar French philosophical environment as comprising "a great variety of existentialists and of philosophers of action, person or spirit, whose approach is similar to existentialism, flanked on the one side by the realism and intellectualism of the Thomists and on the other side by the dialectical materialism of the Marxists." The French philosopher Wahl boiled down this analysis even further. Amid the many voices, he recognized only three major groups—the Catholics (dominated by the neo-Thomists who were the official spokespeople for Catholic thought), the Communists, and the existentialists.[46] Idealistic, nominalistic, and naturalistic thought had virtually disappeared from French philosophical discourse during this period and the analytic tradition was almost nonexistent.[47]

This structuring of the postwar community may have helped Sartreanism to flourish. The strength of the two opposing schools of orthodox Marxism and neo-Thomism and the uncompromising nature of their ideas may have made Sartreanism a resting place for people eager to have an ideology but alienated by party-line Marxism and neo-Thomism because of the unfaltering allegiance that these schools required. Sartreanism also attracted attention immediately after the war because of the value placed on literature as an appropriate philosophical medium. French philosophers certainly quarreled with Sartre's ideas, but his use of literary means to convey them was not widely questioned. The worlds of philosophy and literature were closely linked in postwar France.[48]

In summary, the French philosophical community supported the burgeoning of Sartreanism in diverse ways. Acceptance of particular themes was important but so was controversy; disagreement as well as consensus propelled Sartre into the philosophical limelight. Sartre's ideas were buoyed up by the simultaneous blossoming of movements like phenomenology, Hegelian revivalism, and humanistic Marxism. And the overarching structure of a philosophical community with Marxism and neo-Thomism as two monumental schools of thought created a need for a more flexible philosophy. Finally, Sartreanism's intertwinement with the world of French politics and literature enlarged its sphere of influence. In America, Sartreanism would encounter an altogether different philosophical soil.

2

Mostly Skepticism
American Philosophers' Initial
Response to Sartreanism, 1945–1947

American philosophers' initial contact with Sartre's ideas and the early opinions they formed established many of the enduring contours of their postwar response to French existentialism. Philosophers' first brush with early Sartreanism—that strand of atheistic existentialism that focused on choice as the irreducible expression of individual freedom and the contingency of human existence—occurred in widely different contexts in the period of early acquaintanceship between 1945 and 1947. A very few heard about this philosophy while serving as soldiers in Europe, but most became aware of Sartreanism at home, after the war was over.

Within academia French literature departments rather than philosophy departments usually initiated the introduction to Sartreanism.

This was primarily due to French literature professors' prior knowledge of Sartre as a novelist and playwright and to their greater fluency in French. William Barrett, then an editor of the *Partisan Review* and a philosophy instructor at both Columbia University and New York University, was the only American philosopher during these years of initiation to recommend in print that colleagues investigate Sartreanism. Barrett explained in *Partisan Review* essays such as "What Is Existentialism?" that this particular strain of existentialism bore watching because of its insistence on reintegrating the centrality of human experience into philosophical inquiry.[1]

Most philosophers first learned about Sartre by reading accounts in popular newspapers and magazines; a much smaller number attended his American lectures, saw his plays, or delved into his philosophical works; indirect contact was therefore much more important than direct contact.[2] Articles about Sartre were beginning to proliferate in newspapers and in both lowbrow and highbrow magazines, but American philosophers had not written any books or produced many articles on Sartreanism for their professional journals. Before 1948 philosophers' published impressions of Sartreanism were limited, but these impressions reflected the American context the philosophy encountered.

* * *

One of the earliest forms of contact with Sartreanism occurred while Americans served as soldiers in World War II, yet only a few philosophers received their introduction in this way. Robert Cumming, later a Columbia University professor and a Sartre scholar, discovered the French philosophy while he was a soldier in the French army; Stuart Brown, a philosopher at Cornell who enlisted in the U.S. Army Signal Corps, tried unsuccessfully to contact Sartre while he was stationed in Paris after the German surrender.[3] Some Americans who entered other academic fields came to Sartreanism in like fashion. Robert Cohn, who later studied existentialism under Henri Peyre at Yale and eventually became a professor of French literature at Stanford, read Sartre's literary works while completing military service in France. But his interest then, he has written, was "only in passing since I was involved in other matters—the war, raw life."[4] Those who were introduced to Sartre's ideas as soldiers had little time to ponder them until the battles were over. When they returned to America to resume educations and careers, a slight familiarity sometimes blossomed into a compelling interest.

American philosophers had small chance to study Sartre during the war, nor did they learn much about him in France in the next two years. Few American philosophy students studied in European institutions until they began to take advantage of the Fulbright fellowship program in 1949, three years after its beginning.[5] And even if they had entered European universities between 1945 and 1947, they would have made little contact with Sartreanism there. Sartreanism was considered a "café philosophy," discussed in the social gathering places of French intellectuals but not yet taught in the schools, largely because its illogical overtones ran contrary to the strong current of Cartesian rationalism that dominated French academic philosophy.

Philosophy professors and students within American academia were not primarily responsible for the introduction of Sartre's work; members of French literature departments played a much more important role. They were supportive of Sartre's concept of an "engaged literature" in which authors used novels and plays as vehicles to address contemporary social and political issues, and they also appreciated the technical quality of Sartre's best literary works. Certainly, close contact with French philosophical and cultural developments made these literature departments likely American magnets, and the ability of people in the field to read original works easily increased the likelihood that they would be familiar with him before less fluent French readers were. There were no translations of Sartre's major philosophical works in the initial stage of contact; as we shall see, this naturally impeded Sartre's introduction to the philosophical community. The availability in English of such plays and novels as *The Flies* (1947), *No Exit* (1947), *The Age of Reason* (1947), and *The Reprieve* (1947) and the inaccessibility in English of Sartre's major philosophical works encouraged people to consider Sartreanism primarily as a literary school.[6]

Sartreanism's single most important port of entry into America in the mid-1940s was the Yale French department, due to the presence there of Cohn, Kenneth Douglas, and Peyre, department chairperson. Cohn, then one of Peyre's graduate students, spearheaded the drive to introduce Sartreanism into the Yale curriculum by requesting a course on existentialism. One of those who had become sketchily acquainted with Sartre's ideas during the war, Cohn hoped to expand his knowledge, and he recognized that there was a "market" for Sartreanism; he knew that there were avidly interested faculty members and that they might "have something to say about this fascinating new movement to a public already eager for the news." Peyre fully supported the class that Cohn proposed, and it was offered in 1946—one of the first courses to discuss Sartre on an American college campus. Douglas, another member of the department, asked to teach the class because he had been interested in the topic for some time, and Peyre and other faculty members offered additional courses in later years. Cohn never forgot Douglas's extreme enthusiasm for his subject. He remembered Douglas as "a remarkable Irishman . . . who had gone to Germany as an actor before World War II and had studied existentialism with [Karl] Jaspers and had gone on to read Sartre *et al.*"[7]

Peyre, department chairperson from 1939 to 1969 and a literary critic with an international reputation, was the first professor in any American college to enthusiastically encourage the scholarly study of Sartre. He actively channeled his students toward an examination of French existentialism as a literary and philosophical movement of consequence. A French native, Peyre graduated from the École Normale Supérieure the year Sartre entered it. Peyre was very favorably impressed in 1938 by the originality of *La Nausée*—a novel written in the form of a diary in which the main character vividly experiences the contingency of existence—and he continued to follow Sartre's work closely throughout the war.[8]

Peyre and many of his colleagues were impressed by Sartre's idea of a literature that asserted the duty of writers to voice their political scruples and hopes for a rebuilt world, and they valued the literary skill embedded in Sartre's best efforts. Another factor that attracted them to Sartre was French writers' own attraction to American authors such as Ernest Hemingway, John Dos Passos, and William Faulkner; that interest presented students of French literature with another angle of vision from which to understand their subject. Peyre invited Sartre to lecture at Yale when he learned that the philosopher would be one of seven French journalists brought over by the Office of War Information to report on the national war effort. Later Peyre remembered that "we were all, in the Yale French Department, keenly interested in existentialism, gave courses on it, raved about *Huis Clos, Les Mouches.*" Sartre delivered two lectures at Yale in April 1945; the first dealt with philosophy, and the second with literature.[9]

Cohn, Douglas, and Peyre were the main carriers of Sartrean thought at Yale. This was natural because of their professional literary interests and their appreciation of Sartre's mastery of satire and epic humor, his avoidance of some of the pitfalls of didactic literature, and his intelligent assimilation of the American novel. His philosophy attracted them because of its exploration of nothingness, contingency, freedom, absurdity, and its rejection of any form of determinism.[10] For Douglas, prior knowledge of German existentialism was an additional factor. As we shall see, some American philosophers who investigated Sartreanism also did so because they were already conversant with other strains of thought, particularly the German varieties. Of course Peyre was a likely conduit because he was French; his knowledge of French culture and his ability to understand the many nuances of Sartreanism made him a natural importer.

French natives played key roles in transporting Sartre's ideas to America both because of the attraction of his ideas and because their cultural heritage and linguistic ability made importation easy. They were attuned to the subtleties of meaning embedded in Sartre's work, and they could get beneath the surface of Sartreanism and explain its historical roots and contemporary relevance. They were aware, too, of the intellectual currents of Cartesian rationalism, neo-Hegelianism, and Marxism that crosscut the French philosophy and of Sartreanism's role as a philosophical alternative to Thomism or Marxism. Wahl, the visiting French existentialist and poet who taught philosophy at major American universities during the war years, illustrated the importance of the French native's role. He produced the first article on Sartreanism published by a philosopher in an American magazine.

During the initial wave of Sartreanism's popularity in Paris, Wahl wrote "Existentialism: A Preface," an essay in the *New Republic* designed to demystify the philosophical roots of Sartreanism for those Americans who were having difficulty differentiating Sartre's ideas from other existentialist strains. As Wahl noted, "There is much talk in Paris, in Greenwich Village, even in the center of Manhattan, about existence and existentialism." After pointing out Sartre's kinship with, and divergence from, Heidegger's *Existenz* philosophy, Wahl boiled down Sartreanism to a body of thought that emphasized the difference between human beings and things: "[Man] is for himself, and this inadequacy produces in him a kind of disgust before the too numerous things in themselves, and a kind of fright before the thing for itself which he is and is not."[11] This distillation emphasized early Sartreanism's forceful assertion of the individual's involvement in a world that combined intellectual constructions amenable to rational control and less brute existence.

Rather than read about Sartreanism, some American philosophers might have chosen to attend his lectures, but few did so. Sartre traveled twice to the United States in these years, and his main task on the first trip (from January 1945 to April 1945) was to report on the American war effort. The second trip (from December 1945 to March 1946) was specifically a lecture tour that included Yale, Harvard, Princeton, Columbia, and Carnegie Hall. Interested professors in the French literature departments of these universities arranged his lectures, while the Carnegie Hall speech was organized by Charles Henri Ford, the editor of the short-lived avant-garde literary magazine *View*.[12]

Professional philosophers rarely went to these talks for several reasons. Sartre usually presented his ideas without translators, and many did not easily understand rapidly spoken French. Sartreanism's popularity among writers and members of French literature departments encouraged its identification as a literary movement, and this too dampened philosophers' interest; its escalating literary renown worked to diminish its philosophical reputation. Otto Kraushaar, then a Smith College philosophy professor who became the president of Goucher College in 1949, explained the attitude of many of his colleagues at middecade: "When existentialism first became news, chiefly through the agency of M. Sartre . . . it was a common observation of professional philosophers that here was a typical post-war phenomenon, a literary cult, a fad, which would sputter out."[13] Philosophers also had the opportunity to introduce themselves to Sartre's works by seeing two plays that had been translated by 1947. *No Exit* and *The Flies* appeared on Broadway and on college campuses but, as with Sartre's lectures, philosophers did not attend these plays in any great number.

Contact with Sartre's ideas could also come through reading original works. Here American philosophers were again hampered by their lack of fluency in French. The American educational system's reluctance to support foreign language study adequately has had the effect of delaying the impact of European philosophy, and Sartreanism naturally suffered from this hesitance. Although philosophy departments in the 1950s and 1960s typically required their graduate students to demonstrate "proficiency" in two languages, often the level of skill demanded was not high enough to enable people to easily read works like *L'Être et le néant* that were full of convolutions and idiomatic expressions. New-hall felt that his experience was typical of that of others who earned their degrees in the 1940s and 1950s. Newhall passed the language exam required of him at Princeton by translating two passages from French and German philosophers, but he felt that he would have needed additional language training to easily understand Sartre. Forrest Williams, a Sartre scholar at the University of Colorado, agreed with Newhall; the degree of language proficiency differed greatly among philosophy departments, and sometimes the level of comprehension was not very deep.[14]

The only philosophical study by Sartre available in English in 1947 was *Existentialism,* a short essay based on a very popular lecture, "Existentialisme est un humanisme." This piece was translated into English by Bernard Frechtman, an American who was an intimate of many of the most famous postwar writers in France. Originally published by the New York–based Philosophical Library and sold for a high price that reflected Sartre's current faddishness in literary circles, *Existentialism* focused on ethical questions and reduced key doctrines to phrases that would have a wider appeal. Here Sartre distilled his complex explanation of subjectivity down to the statement that human beings were what they made of themselves—a rejection of any sort of religious, political, or social determinism that denied the individual's ability to choose. In this essay Sartre also presented one of his earliest arguments against the charge that his philosophy had no viable social ethics. He countered that the existentialist position that individuals were responsible for themselves necessarily had ethical ramifications on a societal level because it contained the idea that individuals were also responsible for everyone else. Finally, Sartre simplified his discussion of anguish by presenting it as that moment of recognition when individuals understood that they were ultimately responsible for all their choices and the impact of those choices on other people.[15]

Many philosophers' ability to examine Sartre's ideas in great detail was delayed for thirteen years until *L'Être et le néant* was completely translated in 1956 by Barnes, a philosopher and classics professor at the University of Colorado.[16] Robert Cornish, a graduate student in philosophy at Columbia in the 1950s who was writing a dissertation on French existentialism under Cumming, noted the change that the publication of *Being and Nothingness* produced: "It was only with the translation of *L'Être et le néant* that he [Sartre] began to have any philosophical following."[17] And even after 1956, Cornish recalled, *Being and Nothingness* was rarely read in its entirety. "Only those who had read *Being and Nothingness* are apt to realize that Sartre was a major thinker. . . . All too few have done this."[18] Except for the extremely short philosophical essay, Sartre's treatises have taken an average of fifteen years to be translated into English. The long period between original publication and English versions helped postpone the development of philosophical interest in the United States.

American philosophers' contact with Sartreanism, then, began on a bad note. There was little of it, and what there was did not impress the majority. Of particular importance was the fact that the misbegotten *Existentialism*—an essay Sartre later repudiated as too reductionistic— was long the only translated philosophical work. As Joseph Fell, a Sartre scholar at Bucknell University, has pointed out: "It is unfortunate that the first and only work of Sartre's that most students and many professing philosophers in this country read . . . was the 'Existentialism is a Humanism' lecture—a drastically oversimplified exposition that Sartre himself regrets having published."[19]

* * *

Many American philosophers, along with Americans generally, became acquainted with Sartreanism through newspapers, popular magazines, and journals of opinion such as the *Partisan Review,* the *New Republic,* and the *Nation.* Information about French thought and culture had been almost unattainable during the occupation, and now American journalists were eager to report on, and Americans were anxious to read about, French developments. Although philosophers were not usually receptive to Sartre's ideas, Sartre's philosophy was popular among a small group of intellectuals and writers. Sometimes attracted as much by Sartre's identification with Parisian bohemian life as by his philosophical doctrines, these Americans reproduced Sartre's popularity in France on a smaller scale. A flood of articles on Sartre and existentialism heightened this fad. The columnist Dorothy Norman wrote in the *New York Post:* " 'Avant-garde' magazines all over the country are beginning to bulge with articles by or about the brilliant French writer Jean-Paul Sartre. . . . The anti-Stalinist *Partisan Review* applauds him. The *New Yorker* smiles. The fashion magazines begin to record the Sartre 'trend.' "[20]

While some literary and social commentators expressed strong approval and appreciation of facets of existentialism, the primary response was negative. Repeatedly, Sartre's ideas were viewed as an ephemeral philosophical reflection of war-torn Europe; some commentators linked them more specifically to the romantic tonalities of the French Resistance. During these years of introduction, the majority of observers argued that Sartre's thought was hopelessly pessimistic. Their list of complaints was thorough: It was antiprogress, antiscience, antisocial, and immoral. Sartreanism was also criticized because it was considered politically inert—a philosophy unable to help Europe build a brighter political future.

American commentators regularly expressed variations on the theme that Sartreanism was not a "proper philosophy." One version of this litany was that the philosophy was too intertwined with literary currents; another was that it was a short-lived crisis school spawned by war. What disturbed many critics was Sartreanism's voguishness; some writers heartily disapproved of the coexistence of celebrity and philosopher in Sartre. They envisioned philosophy as a discipline that embodied the highest principles of truth and wisdom, and therefore they believed philosophers should not be associated with popular fads fueled by the values of novelty and entertainment. Sartreanism was also distrusted because it was a "café philosophy" rather than an academic product.

The theme that Sartreanism was an evanescent fad—a philosophical expression of the European political, social, and economic upheaval brought about by World War II—was particularly strong. Although most observers recognized that Sartreanism was also the outgrowth of a long line of philosophical inquiries that became compelling by the middle of the nineteenth century, the idea that it was an intellectual by-product of the war was the stressed motif. *"Existentialism," Time* magazine's first unsigned article on Sartre in 1946, highlighted Sartre's support of the French Resistance and gave a heroic cast to his image.[21]

But Sartreanism's identification with the war had negative connotations as well. Commentators maintained that a doctrine that was so much a mirror of an atypical epoch could have no transcendent significance. The cultural critic and historian Jacques Barzun expressed this view in an article in the *American Scholar* in 1946. It was war, he wrote, that had produced "the thirst for a fresh creed, a new language of belief [that] accounts at least for the intensity if not for the success of the movement."[22] A French native, Barzun was like several other early commentators in America who were likely purveyors of Sartreanism because of their ethnic connections.

Pessimism was another overarching theme in the articles that introduced Americans to Sartre. First reports in both *Harper's* magazine and *Life* expressed this leitmotiv in their titles: "French and American Pessimism" and "Existentialism: Postwar Paris Enthrones a Bleak Philosophy of Pessimism." Oliver Barres, a Yale Divinity School student who later wrote widely on the advantages of ecumenicalism, acknowledged that Sartre strongly denied this negative charge; in a review of *Existentialism* for the *Saturday Review of Literature,* however, Barres flatly declared that "no matter how Jean-Paul Sartre tries to wriggle out of the accusation, his existentialism is a philosophy of despair. *Life*'s first article on Sartre etched the pessimistic verdict into the minds of readers in indelible fashion. In Sartre's philosophy, wrote Bernard Frizell, a novelist and Paris correspondent for *Life,* "man is fearful, cowardly, hesitant, evil, guilty, egotistical, self-enclosed, unapproachable, impure, tragic and worried."[23] A longer list of sorry attributes would be difficult to find.

Sartreanism was also perceived by many American observers during this period as a philosophy that included a worrisome antisocial tone. Barres deplored Sartre's emphasis on individual isolation: "This is man's world, says Sartre, and no one can help him out of it. Here on this mysterious sea of drowning swimmers, arms thrash the water in panic and voices cry out for help, but all in vain." John Lackey Brown, a professor of French at Catholic University before the war who was a Paris correspondent for the *New York Times* between 1945 and 1948, also doubted that the socially disconnected individual whom Sartre described would have much appeal. "Few mortals can live the courageous and hopeless despair preached by Sartre," Brown argued in the *New York Times* article "Paris, 1946: Its Three War Philosophies."[24]

The absence of a well-defined presentation of a positive morality or a clear political path was a closely connected concern. Many recognized that a seed of value lay behind Sartre's assertion of the individual's freedom to choose, but his unwillingness to present this concept as an incontrovertible universal moral good found little American acceptance. In a 1946 article entitled "Politics and the Intellectual," the *Nation*'s European editor, J. Alvarez del Vayo, described Sartreanism as an unsuccessful attempt by philosophers to enter the political arena.[25] In del Vayo's view, Sartreanism was a vaguely leftist ideology that was negative, self-defeating, and unable to replace democratic capitalism with a better system. If it were representative of philosophy's attempt to provide political solutions, del Vayo concluded, the discipline should discontinue its effort to play such a role.

The charge that Sartreanism was not a "proper philosophy" permeated American observations too. Many were distrustful of a doctrine that received so much attention in the popular press. Although the French philosophy was indeed in vogue in Paris and some adherents identified themselves by wearing sleek black clothing or flocking to selected cafés, its appeal was sometimes overblown by reporters who tended to write about the excitement surrounding its faddishness and who neglected to mention the opposition it encountered. Sartre was labeled the "chief prophet," "existentialist in chief," "high priest," or "high prophet"—terms used mockingly to make the distaste for his appeal clear. Sartreanism's popularity among intellectual hangers-on who did not fully understand the concepts rankled American commentators too. The *Life* correspondent Frizell was pleased because Sartre's voguishness signified the return of intellectual vibrancy to Parisian life, but he deplored the lack of understanding: "When recently a student seated himself at a café table and announced that he was going to eat the most enormous meal in history, the comment of onlookers was 'Obviously an existentialist.' "[26]

Sartreanism's development outside of French academic institutions was also suspect. Americans wondered how a serious philosophy could emerge from Parisian cafés. Most did not recognize that these mid–twentieth-century meeting places were, in a sense, analogous to the eighteenth-century French salon. They were places where philosophers, writers, and artists could exchange ideas without confronting head-on the intellectual traditions of academic institutions.[27] By contrast, academic philosophers did not have similar noninstitutional settings in which they could explore the unorthodox ideas of Sartreanism. As we shall see, the philosophy later found one of its first American homes in the off-campus coffee houses and other meeting places of students that identified themselves as intellectuals and artists in the late 1950s and early 1960s. Physical settings—with all their social and intellectual ramifications—helped diminish or intensify interest in Sartreanism.

Embedded in the theme that Sartreanism was not a legitimate doctrine was criticism that it was a literary movement rather than a philosophical one. John Lackey Brown evaluated this interpretation in

"Chief Prophet of Existentialism," an important feature story on Sartre published in the *New York Times Magazine* in 1947 that demonstrated readers' curiosity and interest in the topic.[28] Although Brown knew that Sartre considered his literary works an inseparable part of his philosophy, Brown concluded that Sartreanism might be more properly classified as a literary movement because many of Sartre's philosophical studies went unread while his literary works were very popular. Because knowledgeable observers like Brown often emphasized Sartreanism's literary connections, philosophers were not encouraged to take it seriously as a philosophy. Most of the commentators also added that Sartreanism lacked philosophical precision, a complaint that continually reverberated in later years. Some contended that the arguments were not tightly constructed; major concepts like *being* and *nothingness,* upon which the entire philosophy depended, they claimed, were ambiguously formulated. "Existentialism is difficult to define," wrote Frizell, "and is clothed by its followers in yards of all but impenetrable jargon."[29]

Just as commentators offered an essentially negative view of Sartre's ideas, some also presented Sartre himself in a hostile light. Several were discomfited by his physical appearance. In an anonymous *Time* spoof, Sartre was described as the "wall-eyed little founder of existentialism." And Frizell remarked in "Existentialism" that "the personality behind the nationwide excitement over existentialism is a short, ugly, wall-eyed individual named Jean-Paul Sartre."[30] When the philosopher arrived at the Waldorf-Astoria Hotel in a plaid lumberjack jacket to begin his first tour of America, a tailor was quickly ushered in to provide less "bohemian" clothing.[31]

Sartre's political attacks on the United States provided a more substantive source of disapproval. Although he was appreciative of American military support during the war and was less opposed to U.S. foreign policy between 1945 and 1947 than he would be in subsequent years, Sartre was still outspoken when he thought American actions were harmful. The first *New York Times* story to focus on Sartre, "De Gaulle Foes Paid by U.S., Paris Is Told," written by John Lackey Brown, reported accusations Sartre made against the State Department and the American business community.[32] Writing in the French paper *Figaro,* Sartre contended that American officials and businesspeople had bribed French émigrés to print anti-Gaullist literature.

In a letter to the *Times* responding to Brown's article, Sartre charged that Brown misunderstood the context in which Sartre had criticized Americans. Sartre's letter reflected his characteristic political stance—a blend of accusations against American capitalism and appreciation of American military assistance during World War II that was often difficult for others to fathom. In one breath Sartre announced that "my only desire is to continue . . . to create durable bonds between our countries," but in another he accused Americans of bribery.[33] Sartre's contentions may have been valid, but they were unproven. They certainly did not help to establish a positive relationship between Sartre and Americans who did not agree that the only motive behind American foreign aid to France was the desire to control the French economy and political life. The French philosopher's appraisal of American culture followed his political tendency to combine strong criticism with carefully measured approval, a pattern in which the attack was often more memorable than the praise. Sartre continued this perplexing pattern in "Americans and Their Myths," an article for the *Nation* in 1947. He complimented the American people on many counts but concluded that they were in "cultural anguish" because they wanted both to escape and embrace the myth that this was the land of unlimited opportunity.[34]

Sartre's bohemianism rankled some commentators too. He was often presented either as an individual with a questionable "bohemian tendency" or as a bourgeois masquerading as a bohemian—allusions to Sartre's enjoyment of drinking, partying, and sexual adventures. In his article "Chief Prophet of Existentialism," John Lackey Brown described the prewar years as "the bohemian period of existentialism"—an age of scandal in which sunbathing in the nude and listening to American jazz had been favorite pastimes. Sartre was also scorned for succumbing to bourgeois ambitions in "Pursuit of Wisdom: Existentialism, Lettrism and Sensorialism," an anonymous *Time* article: "Sartre was an international figure; he was making money: he was planning to open a play in New York . . . the bohemian tradition was being betrayed."[35]

In the final analysis, American faultfinding with Sartre was inseparable from the charges against Sartreanism as a philosophy. The accusation that Sartre was a bohemian—a Left Bank intellectual who lacked academic legitimacy—was part of the judgment that Sartreanism was not a proper philosophy because it did not emerge from a university. Distrust of Sartre because of his quarrels with American foreign policy and culture went hand in hand with the recognition that Sartreanism was, in some ways, antithetical to the perception of American culture as one that embodied an affirmation of optimism, pragmatism, science, and rational progress. Finally, the contention that Sartre was a disreputable figure because he was a philosopher who made money from the popularity of his ideas helped produce the verdict that Sartreanism was spurious.

Sparingly scattered throughout Americans' commentary, however, was the important recognition that Sartre's ideas spoke very forcefully to the individual's sense of self in the mid–twentieth century. The *Time* correspondent Frizell emphasized that Sartre posed the "fundamental question of our times"—what should be done about the miserable state of the modern world in which individuals felt abandoned and helpless? And John Lackey Brown stressed that no matter how much it was a product of World War II, Sartre's thought was not static, but a philosophy whose evolution definitely bore watching. Brown followed Sartre's struggle to reconcile his concepts of individual liberty, political solidarity, and the absence of moral absolutes carefully during these years, and he deeply appreciated Sartre's willingness to tackle the most difficult issues of his era.[36]

Occasionally, commentators even saw Sartre's professional unorthodoxy in a positive light. At the Yale Divinity School, Barres argued that Sartre's distance from the academy gave him a more honest view of the intimate anxieties of contemporary existence: "Sartre is no library philosopher. . . . He is at least a life in motion and will have no truck with static balcony views. For him reality cannot be understood by the analytical speculations of withdrawn minds but only as it strikes home."[37] In sum, the impressions that appeared in the newspapers and magazines that provided most American philosophers with their first contact with Sartreanism were predominately negative. Within this largely hostile framework, however, an appreciation of Sartre's emphasis on the irreducibility of the individual and the travails of mid–twentieth-century life sometimes survived.

* * *

How did American philosophers respond to this strain of existentialism in the years of first acquaintanceship between 1945 and 1947? The most striking characteristic of the American reaction, in comparison to the French, was simply that Sartreanism was a much less important and volatile movement in the American community. The reasons for this range from the practical to the philosophical.

Americans did not experience the volume of existentialist works that the French did, nor the rapidity of the production of new books and articles in such a short period of time. And coverage by the American press was, of course, not as extensive as French reportage. More important, the intellectual landscape of American philosophy had different contours. Although a few Americans shared particular interests with French philosophers, the combination and strength of concerns in the two milieus were very dissimilar. In France, knowledge of other strains of Continental existentialism, as well as a strong interest in phenomenology, neo-Hegelianism, humanistic Marxism, and greater sympathy for the use of literature as a philosophical medium, helped to create a very nurturing environment. In America, as we shall see, the currents of naturalism, pragmatism, realism, and analytic philosophy converged to create a more unsympathetic community.

The United States also lacked the social and political setting that buoyed Sartreanism in France. Sartre's cultural significance in France was rooted, in part, in his expression of the social and political needs that arose out of French guilt and disillusion emanating from the war years. By contrast, Americans had not gone through the demoralizing experience of defeat or enemy occupation. America's national power was affirmed in World War II, not called into question. In comparison with the French, Americans in the two-year period following the war were less morally bereft, less desperate to design a new national ethic. Although most responded positively to Sartre's call for a morality that accentuated individual freedom and responsibility—both because these ideals had a long tradition and because their importance was heightened by the perception that America's role in World War II made it responsible for the global survival of freedom—Americans initially were less attentive to Sartreanism than were the French. When the ideological strife of the Cold War intensified after 1947 and concerns about loss of individuality escalated, Sartreanism's moral inquiries and impasses would have a great deal more resonance.

* * *

What was the general response of American philosophers to Sartre? The few who did comment on Sartre's ideas in print in this initial stage had much to say about the reactions of their quiet colleagues. Like the magazine and newspaper commentators, many professional philosophers viewed Sartreanism as an evanescent postwar mood that revealed no universal truths. Although the metaphysician Justus Buchler, then a new addition to the philosophy department at Columbia, was certainly not favorably disposed toward Sartreanism when he reviewed *Existentialism* in 1947 in the *Nation,* he felt it necessary to remind colleagues: "To call it a mere reflection of modern confusion, as some responsible persons have done, seems at best an oversimplification." Buchler also found value in the attention Sartre paid to the moral categories of despair, absurdity, and the choice of oneself.[38]

Associated with this perception that Sartreanism was simply a postwar phenomenon was the familiar verdict that Sartre's thought was too pessimistic, too much a mirror of the war. Barrett, one of the few American philosophers of this period to actively encourage colleagues to consider the merits of existentialism, believed that American philosophers' negative response was partly the result of the persistence of optimism in the national ethos. Sartreanism's "very somberness went against the grain of our native youthfulness and optimism," Barrett later observed in his 1958 philosophical and sociological exposition of existentialism, *Irrational Man: A Study in Existential Philosophy.*[39] The old theme of American confidence contrasted to European despair and world-weariness, he concluded, had surfaced once again in the response to Sartre. Barrett, who became an assistant professor at New York University in 1948, continued to serve on the editorial board of the *Partisan Review.* Like other *Partisan Review* editors, he was eager to introduce Americans to new currents circulating in Europe, and the ideas of intellectuals like Sartre filled the pages of the magazine in these years. To satisfy the demand for information on existentialism, Barrett wrote "What Is Existentialism?" and *Partisan Review* published it as a separate pamphlet in 1947.

Sartre's opposition to specialization was another source of disapproval among philosophers, and in "What Is Existentialism?" Barrett aligned himself with Sartre and went against the prospecialization tide in America. For the most part, academic philosophy had become specialized philosophy in the United States by midcentury.[40] Although many American philosophers fought the current in the 1940s—in fact this was a period when some philosophers worried among themselves that their inquiries were becoming too narrow in scope—the specializing trend was definitely increasing, fueled by the prestige of scientific methodology with its emphasis on well-defined parameters.[41] Barrett's opposition to specialization provided an excellent ground for his appreciation of existentialism. He applauded the existentialists for adopting a methodology that broadened the philosophical data under consideration to include new sources of human feeling and experience.[42] For many Americans then, Sartreanism was too "antispecialization," and therefore too "antiscience," to be taken seriously. Sartre's opposition to sociological and psychological models that dissected individuals into discrete parts and did not grapple with the totality of human experience, and his complaints about analytic philosophy because of its tendency to reduce the field of vision, put Sartre squarely in the camp of those who feared overspecialization.

The American philosophical community was also suspicious of the coverage Sartre received in the popular media. Though Barrett was pleased that Sartreanism had encouraged discussion outside academic circles, even he conceded that the faddishness surrounding French existentialism "created a certain embarrassment in some of us."[43] Professionals were understandably skeptical when articles on Sartre appeared in fashion magazines like *Harper's Bazaar*.[44] This negative association with cultural voguishness of course did not prohibit philosophers from investigating Sartreanism further; it simply set up an additional barrier that made it more unlikely that they would do so.

Philosophers reiterated the view that Sartreanism was fundamentally a literary movement. Sartre's American introduction by way of enthusiasts of French literature, and the initial translation of his plays and novels rather than of his major philosophical works, helped enhance his literary importance at the expense of his philosophical standing. An element of professional jealousy and territorialism surfaced here; Sartreanism was "interdisciplinary" in a period when the currents of specialization and professionalization ran counter to such an approach.

Equally significant in this consigning of Sartre to the realm of literature was many philosophers' verdict that he simply did not respect the canons of philosophical argumentation. His success, concluded the Columbia University professor Buchler, "has been in narrative, semibiographical and dramatic contexts, where standards of explication and rigor are irrelevant." Marjorie Grene, the first American philosopher to produce a monograph on Sartre (*Dreadful Freedom: A Critique of Existentialism* [1948]), complained in the 1947 *Kenyon Review* essay "L'Homme est une passion inutile: Sartre et Heidegger" that Sartre was "arguing, extremely cleverly, but in Plato's sense sophistically: with the end of persuasion not of truth." She protested what she thought was Sartre's willingness to sidestep any logical constraints that undermined his central ideas. Barrett, too, joined in this critique even though he was one of existentialism's staunchest supporters. *L'Être et le néant,* wrote Barrett, was "so philosophically naive, abounds in such bad philosophical arguments, inconclusive arguments offered as conclusive—that we find it difficult to reconcile Sartre's obvious acuteness with his extreme naiveté, and positive obtuseness."[45]

As these philosophers' observations reveal, considerable agreement existed between opinions outside and within the philosophical community. This was to be expected when few philosophers were able or willing to make more direct contact with the intricacies of Sartre's doctrines. Ideas about Sartreanism in this period of acquaintanceship were affected by the hearsay evidence that appeared in newspapers and magazines. And, of course, some of the opinions contained seeds of truth. Sartreanism was, in part, tied to the social context of war-damaged Europe just as any body of thought has necessary connections to its historical environment, and *L'Être et le néant* was a philosophical treatise that did contain flights of fancy and illogical arguments. There was a good bit of poetic imagination on display, for example, in Sartre's discussion of eating as an appropriation of being. He maintained that the food one chose reflected the particular mode of being—essentially active or passive—that individuals selected as their original project or fundamental self-definition: "It is not a matter of indifference whether we like oysters or clams, snails or shrimp, if only we know how to unravel the existential significance of these foods."[46] It may not have been a matter of indifference but clearly Sartre was overinterpreting the phenomena.

Few American philosophers published systematic observations on Sartre between 1945 and 1947 due to the influence of the language barrier, professional boundaries, and perspectives about what constituted legitimate philosophical inquiry. Most of the commentary was elicited by the obligation to review the newly translated *Existentialism* in 1947. Barrett, Buchler, Grene, Kraushaar, and Roy Sellars—a critical realist at the University of Michigan—revealed agreements and disagreements among American philosophers when they offered their evaluations. One of the most repeated complaints of these observers was that Sartreanism failed to place the individual within the world of sense data and that Sartre therefore trivialized the importance of a scientific perspective.

Sartre's thought was considered overly dependent on a phenomenological method that viewed nature and the world of objects exclusively from the vantage point of human consciousness. Philosophers disapproved of the absence of any attempt to apply scientific methodology aimed at objectivity or of any effort to utilize scientific theories to explain phenomena. Kraushaar summed up this criticism when he objected that Sartreanism was "a truncated, negative mode of thought that embodies all the morbid, arbitrary, subjective, and radical anti-rationalism of Kierkegaard, without defining any point of reference outside of the individual." Buchler elaborated on this point by noting Sartreanism's loss of the "sense of fact" and suggested that the existentialists' "existence" was a subjectively created "mythology." And even Barrett declared: "In the hands of Sartre, French existentialism has become all too phenomenological."[47] In short, the phenomenological method used by Sartre was perceived as unable to transcend the perceptual limitations of a solitary observer.

Influential schools in American philosophy accepted the integration of the realm of nature and consciousness in philosophical systems as fundamental; the idea was embedded in naturalism, pragmatism, and realism. This aspect of a "naturalistic temper" was particularly significant in the rejection of Sartreanism by many philosophers because of naturalism's enduring influence in the mid-1940s.[48] Buchler's wry observation that "it will not be to the existentialists that one would ascribe mastery of fact" was indicative of the naturalistically minded response.[49] Like many others, Buchler protested that existentialists set up human existence and human values in a realm distinct from material being.

The clash between the linguistic characteristics of existentialist thought and those of analytic philosophy was also brought to light. Analytic philosophy—an umbrella term for philosophical schools that developed in the early decades of the twentieth century from the linguistic, logical, mathematical, and scientific analyses of philosophy initiated by G. E. Moore, Bertrand Russell, and the logical positivists of the Vienna Circle—was a growing force in American philosophy by the mid-1940s; a significant element of the analytic temper was the tendency to approach philosophy through the dissection of language. Edwin Burtt, a graduate of Union Theological Seminary and a philosophy professor at Cornell whose specialties were religious thought and metaphysics, noted the influence of linguistic analysis. Asked in 1952 to pinpoint the major changes in American philosophy between 1900 and 1950, Burtt stressed that: "[T]he outstanding revolution in the field of academic philosophy is reflected in the current emphasis on the field of semantics. . . . Issues that used to be discussed in other terms are now being dealt with as semantic questions."[50]

Barrett recognized that the existentialists' sense and use of language was antithetical to American philosophers' adoption of the linguistic standards of analytic philosophy. In the process of struggling to express the reality of individual existence, existentialists created new and strange terminology, while contemporaries of the analytic persuasion searched for greater precision in language. Although existentialism and analysis presented a united front against rationalism, the two currents were going in opposite directions linguistically. Barrett was very aware of the seriousness of the developing polarity: "Philosophers in one group have largely ceased to understand those in the other," he wrote in "What Is Existentialism?"[51]

The majority of the philosophers who reviewed *Existentialism* agreed that Sartre was too fond of psychologizing. Sellars, a leading exponent of critical realism at the University of Michigan and a rigorously independent thinker, put it bluntly: "Existentialism . . . indulges in subjective, semi-psychological explorations of the crisis of self-consciousness."[52] For Sartre, what appeared to some as "psychologizing" was a necessary philosophical step toward apprehending the basis of human being; the core of human experience was disclosed only in psychologically traumatic encounters, especially life-and-death situations.

Americans, however, rarely accepted the validity of this approach to their discipline. Instead, Sartre was interpreted as focusing on unusual and arresting events that should have been left in the hands of psychologists and psychiatrists. Grene objected to his line of inquiry as unbalanced: "[T]aking Sartre's writing as a whole, one senses . . . a love of exploring to the limits the extreme or perverse in human nature." Sartreanism, Grene concluded with dismay, seemed to "feed on perverseness."[53]

Sartre's ethics also came under loud attack. Sartre presented some first steps toward a morality in *Existentialism*. He argued that when individuals chose they chose for all humanity, and he assumed that individuals chose what they thought was good for themselves, and that what was good for one was good for all. Although there was no clearly demarcated realm of preestablished values in this morality, there was a universal human condition of "choosing the good" that individuals considered when they made decisions; "the good" was the act of choosing individual freedom.[54]

Kraushaar found the idea that a person created universal values through individual choice to be a harbinger of anarchism. For Kraushaar, such a concept opened the door to passion and instinct as arbiters of moral conduct. Buchler noted that Sartre's ethic needed much greater development before it could be taken seriously. With the exception of Barrett, all the philosophers were distressed by Sartre's failure to integrate group dynamics fully into the framework. Grene protested that Sartre's individuals were never "concerned with the universal implications of their acts . . . but only with the awful implications of that freedom—for themselves."[55]

Despite these major criticisms, however, philosophers and other American observers found particular aspects of Sartrean thought compelling. They responded positively to Sartre's opposition to speculative reason and to his recognition of the uncertainty surrounding the doctrine of rational progress in political liberalism. Sartre's interest in uncovering the influence of mass society on the interior of the life of the individual and his emphasis on freedom and responsibility also found an appreciative audience.

The rejection of traditional rationalistic metaphysics met with varied reactions among these philosophers. Sartre's critique was, in a certain sense, a form of "disappointed rationalism." When he argued that neither reality nor individual existence could be understood within a system that presented reason as the source of form and order, he did not question rationalism itself but only rejected the assumption that existence could be fully explained within a rationalistic framework.[56] Nevertheless, Sartre did question the dominion of reason. Of the five American philosophers who first commented on Sartreanism, only Kraushaar was extremely worried by Sartre's "irrationalism." Kraushaar argued for the importance of preserving a belief in reason both within the discipline of philosophy and in the social world. To buoy his own faith in rational progress, Kraushaar fell back on the argument that Sartreanism was primarily the expression of the irrationality of an atypical epoch.[57]

For the other four philosophers, the French thinker's denial of the consistent forward motion of rational progress had more appeal. Faith in rationalistic metaphysics had already been shaken both by contemporary philosophical perspectives and by the historical context of depressions and war when Sartreanism emerged as an additional opponent. Transplanted members of the Vienna Circle—a school that surfaced in the late 1920s in Vienna that set aside metaphysics as nonsense and stressed the importance of the introduction of a well-defined technical vocabulary and the full use of logical methodology—also undermined the validity of rationalistic metaphysics. By focusing on language and the logic of science as philosophy's real core, Rudolf Carnap at the University of Chicago, Hans Reichenbach at the University of California, Berkeley, and other followers of a more analytic persuasion opposed an emphasis on reason as it had been traditionally conceived.

The extent to which American philosophers in general no longer believed in the rule of reason is difficult to assess. Certainly, the idea that human history was a form of evolutionary growth from less rational to more rational activity was beleaguered in the 1940s, but it remained more tenable than it would become in the 1950s when additional wars and ideological conflict would make it even harder to accept. That most of these philosophers found Sartre's rejection of rational progress worthy of consideration suggested a growing tide of disbelief. For American philosophers, Sartre was a contemporary spokesperson for the foundering of rationalistic metaphysics. In political terms, this translated into an assault on the tenet of necessary social progress embedded in liberalism.

All five philosophers had high praise for Sartre's reinforcement of the ideas that the individual had a certain freedom to choose and an obligation to choose responsibly. They validated the ethic of freedom and duty that Sartre championed but was unwilling to acknowledge as a universal value. Even Kraushaar, who so forthrightly challenged Sartreanism, conceded: "[I]t will be no mean accomplishment if existentialism helps agonized modern man to see that he is free in this world of his own making and what that freedom entails."[58]

The staunch manner in which American philosophers agreed with Sartre's insistence on individual liberty suggested that, even if the idea that enlightened democratic political activity would always be able to produce social progress was losing ground, liberalism's advocacy of individual rights had staying power. Kraushaar applauded existentialism's emphasis on human freedom as "its deepest motive, deeper than the subjectivism and irrationalism by which it is more often characterized," but he also strongly disapproved of what he perceived as the debilitating subjectivism that Sartre attached to his portrayal of freedom.[59] He complained that Sartre paid too little attention to the limits nature and society inflicted on the actions of human beings. Sartrean thought, then, related in conflicting ways with the basic tenets of liberalism. On the one hand, Sartreanism rejected the belief in the inevitability of social progress but, on the other hand, it strongly endorsed individual liberty. Between 1945 and 1947 the relationship between liberalism and Sartre's doctrines was just beginning to be explored; in subsequent years it would be pondered in more detail.

Although American philosophers complained that Sartre took little notice of the world as a realm integrating nature, objects, individual existence, and social being, they did respond positively to his effort to understand social interaction through the vantage point of the individual. These philosophers praised Sartre for recognizing that increasingly bureaucratic and technological societies tended to produce a sense of social alienation and loss of personal identity. Sartre was attempting to view thought as a process responding to the social world in which one lived—a philosophical perspective that had a rich heritage in American philosophy and that had surfaced most recently in pragmatism. While philosophers criticized Sartre for not envisioning the human environment in the same way they did—they would have preferred him not to focus so exclusively on individual consciousness but to place the human being within the totality of existence—they applauded his attention to the difficulties of mass society for the individual. In that vein Buchler pinpointed a sense of purposelessness and estrangement from meaningful activities as common contemporary problems in complex industrial societies and praised existentialists because they "have caught forcefully the great fact of tragedy in modern life."[60]

Philosophers who discussed Sartreanism in print in this early period certainly did not agree on its enduring value. Barrett was the only outspoken advocate of existentialism, and even he found important bones to pick. But Barrett also worked hard to establish existentialism's validity by aligning it with a century-long effort in philosophy to place individual existence at the center of inquiry. In the *Partisan Review* article "What Is Existentialism?" Barrett explained that existentialism was a current that crossed lines drawn between philosophical schools and that involved "the whole Western mind . . . bending before a new climate of opinion." Barrett, however, also expressed his uncertainty about the ultimate worth of a movement that needed so much more explication of its ontology and ethics and that seemed to Barrett politically incorrect because it veered too close to an acceptance of Stalinism. Barrett lamented in a review of *L'Être et le néant* and *L'Age de raison* in the *Partisan Review* in 1946 that the novel afforded "the painful revelation that Sartre is well along the road to Stalinism."[61]

What he valued most in existentialism Barrett also considered its greatest weakness. Existentialism's strength was its focus on the centrality of the human being as the creator of a philosophy, but this same intensive focus on human subjectivity, Barrett concluded, allowed only a partial understanding of reality. In the final analysis, Barrett had not yet reconciled opposing perceptions of existentialism in his own mind. He was clear, however, about his desire to pursue existentialist inquiries, and he acted on that wish both by teaching courses on existentialism at New York University and by writing extensive commentary on Sartre. His explorations later culminated in the major work that found a large audience outside his professional circle—*Irrational Man: A Study in Existential Philosophy* (1958). More American philosophers had recognized fruitful lines of thought in existentialism by the time that *Irrational Man* was published, but in the mid-1940s Barrett was virtually the only prophet of this later realization. In very understated fashion, he observed in 1947 regarding existentialism: "It will be interesting to see what comes of this."[62]

"Interesting, one suspects, as a machine gun in the hands of a baboon is interesting," retorted Kraushaar in a 1947 book review of Robert Bretall's *A Kierkegaard Anthology*, Sartre's *Existentialism*, and Barrett's "What Is Existentialism?" in the *Journal of Philosophy*. Of the five philosophers under consideration, Kraushaar produced the most passionately hostile critique. For Kraushaar, Sartre's thought remained a dangerous philosophical derailment that threatened to replace reason with instinct and irrationality. The existentialism of Kierkegaard, Kraushaar observed, at least tried to save the individual from meaningless subjectivity through a saving leap into religion, but Sartre's rejection of this form of faith left Sartreanism only a negative mode of thought. Kraushaar sketched existentialism as a "declaration of independence from the bondage of life to machines, traditions, ideologies, abstractions, [and] the fatalism of history," and noted that as a statement of protest against the rigidity of these social constructions, it had value. But documents of revolt must be followed by some sort of constitution, said Kraushaar, if freedom were not to evaporate. The Smith professor could see no "constitution" in Sartreanism: "Unless that sense of freedom is accompanied by the less spectacular labor of defining the concrete sharable objectives of free men, it will only be a leap from the frying pan into the fire."[63]

The conclusions of Buchler of Columbia University and Sellars of the University of Michigan were less dramatic. They believed Sartreanism was a relatively minor current whose significance was largely limited to France. Buchler argued that the doctrine was primarily a literary movement that would succeed only if it shed itself of any philosophical pretensions. Sellars felt that Sartreanism's importance lay in the evidence it gave of the rejuvenation of French thought, and in its challenge to the philosophical restrictions on human freedom and choice that Thomism and Stalinist Marxism implied.[64]

* * *

To summarize, the 1945–47 period revealed many of the characteristics that would continue to mark American philosophers' response to Sartreanism in later years. Of the diverse elements that combined to shape that reaction, one played an especially critical role: the inability of many to read Sartre's most technical works in French. Did this lack of information cause Americans to undervalue Sartre's thought? Absolutely. As Sellars reminded his colleagues: "It is well to remember that Sartre has written a long technical work . . . and has earned the right to popularize his philosophy."[65] Of course, a host of substantive philosophical issues and sociocultural roadblocks were also influential, but the language barrier was a definite hindrance. The extent to which this problem played a role in Americans' skeptical response would only begin to be sorted out when more of Sartre's work became available in English.

The linguistic obstacle that Sartre's ideas confronted in the United States helped to determine who would become a purveyor of Sartreanism. In these "pretranslation" years, philosophers had to read French fluently to understand the intricacies of Sartreanism. This naturally meant an immediate and severe limitation of the number of Americans who would become interested. The language barrier, then, had a selective function in the philosophical community; those inclined to consider Sartreanism seriously tended to be French natives or individuals capable of reading French easily.

In a broader sense, the importation of Sartreanism faced another cultural impediment in America. Sartre's philosophy was part of the larger European movement of Continental existentialism, and to appreciate Sartre's doctrines fully, it was necessary to be well grounded in the works of Hegel, Heidegger, Jaspers, and Husserl. There were certainly American philosophers who had studied all of these Continental philosophers—Grene was one of them—but in the mid-1940s their numbers were not great. By contrast, America's cultural and philosophical ties with Great Britain made it much easier to import new developments in British philosophy. The few American philosophers who were well versed in Continental philosophy, however, tended to pay more attention to Sartreanism; they, too, were likely importers.

American philosophers' perceptions were also undoubtedly affected by the secondhand and somewhat gossipy information on Sartre purveyed by magazines and newspapers. Although accurate in some respects, these characterizations were also full of hyperbole and misinformation. Commentators in the popular press were inclined to accentuate the negative perceptions of extreme pessimism and faddishness, and these hostile impressions sometimes echoed in philosophers' observations. Sartreanism's introduction to academia, largely via professors of French literature, associated the movement closely with that discipline, and that too cast a shadow on Sartreanism within the philosophic community. In an era of specialization and the solidification of professional values in philosophy that included precision in language and scientific methodology, the strong link with literature was detrimental.

The timing of American philosophers' contact with Sartre's ideas affected their reception too. The first few years after the end of World War II resembled a lull before a storm; anticommunism, the ideological strife of the Cold War, and the sociological worries about what appeared to be overconformity and loss of individual identity that surfaced in books like David Riesman's *The Lonely Crowd* and William Whyte's *Organization Man* in the 1950s had not reached full strength yet in the 1940s.[66] Although the issues that Sartre dealt with sparked interest prior to 1948, they lacked the appeal they would later display. Sartre's commitment to freedom, responsibility, and authenticity would resonate more closely with the philosophical, social, and political concerns generated by the Cold War and with fears about the erosion of individuality in highly industrialized and bureaucratic societies in the 1950s.

The critical philosophical problem in this early period was Sartre's neglect of nature and sense data, and the weakness of his social ethics. Other sources of skepticism were Sartre's outspoken opposition to the scientific slant of contemporary Anglo-American philosophy and his objection to the linguistic paradigm of analytic thought. Sartre's image presented an obstacle in the philosophical community too. For some Americans, Sartre may have symbolized the emergence of a new type of philosopher even though other philosophers shared some of the characteristics that made Sartre distinctive. Bertrand Russell, for example, attacked both capitalism and contemporary bourgeois morality and was roundly criticized for this by some American philosophers, but his investigations in logic and mathematics were also widely applauded as pathbreaking steps in analytic philosophy.

Sartre, however, combined more traits contrary to the common image of a professional philosopher. Not only did he skewer capitalism and loudly question conventional morality, he also opposed academic philosophy; professional philosophers disapproved of Sartre's criticisms of traditional philosophical methodology and his own nonacademic status. Sartre was not fully schooled as a university professor; his credentials were incomplete because he was trained to teach only at the lycée level.[67] And Sartre gave allegiance not only to philosophy but to literature as well. Furthermore, he had celebrity status and an avant-garde following that none could match. The combination of these qualities meant that Sartre required some Americans to stretch their image of what constituted appropriate behavior for a professional philosopher.

The contours of the American philosophical response to Sartreanism were already set by the end of these years of first acquaintance. On the whole, the reaction was highly skeptical, resulting not only from philosophical complaints but from social and cultural roadblocks too. Yet positive connections were also established; though few in number, they would become stronger in the following years. The dearth of published philosophical commentary silently but eloquently revealed the many obstacles Sartreanism confronted in the American philosophical community in this early stage of contact. American philosophers scarcely embraced Sartre with open arms; they did not eagerly try to mesh their perspectives with his. Changes in the philosophical landscape in later years, however, encouraged many more philosophers to investigate Sartreanism.

3

A Share of Credibility
The Second Stage, 1948–1952

In the four years following 1947, American philosophers paid increasing attention to Sartreanism. The period from 1948 through 1952 marked a new stage in that response; it was during these years that more American thinkers began to regard Sartreanism as a philosophical endeavor to be taken seriously. This did not mean that many people accepted most of Sartre's doctrines as valid—that was rarely the case— but that his efforts gained credibility as legitimate philosophical inquiry. This new season in Sartrean scholarship began to be recognizable in 1948, the year in which *The Emotions* followed *Existentialism* as Sartre's second philosophical work to appear in English. *The Psychology of the Imagination,* another important early study, was published in 1948 soon after *The Emotions.*[1] These books naturally encouraged criticism as philosophers evaluated them in book reviews.

The publication of the first extended professional debate about the validity of Sartreanism in the pages of a prestigious professional journal signaled the end of this initial period of gaining legitimacy. That lengthy debate represented a coming-of-age rite in the philosophical community; Sartreanism had now been publicly and professionally blessed as worthy of consideration.

These two interwoven events, the translation of additional philosophical works by Sartre and the attendant growth of criticism, stood out as key forces that enabled the American response to evolve to a new level of credibility. But although the added translations were helpful in this regard, they did not eliminate the information gap that plagued Sartreanism; *L'Être et le néant*, Sartre's major work, remained untranslated. Even an outspoken opponent such as the naturalistically minded Sidney Hook noted in his review of *The Emotions* in 1948: "It is a pity that his [Sartre's] more ambitious writings have not yet been made available in English and that the English-speaking public must judge his philosophical views in their literary form rather than in their more systematic form."[2]

While *L'Être et le néant* was the essential explanatory key to Sartrean thought, and the more widespread diffusion of Sartreanism waited upon its translation (as *Being and Nothingness*) in 1956, publication of *The Emotions* and *The Psychology of the Imagination* did give American philosophers the opportunity to see Sartre's philosophical range. In these works Sartre explored the relationship between emotion, imagination, and individual existence. But although a few philosophers studied the two books, they certainly were not avidly read.

Because the linguistic roadblock was still in place, ethnicity remained a factor in the second phase of contact. European philosophers living in the United States still played an important role in Sartrean criticism. Wahl, the French philosopher-poet who introduced the technical underpinnings of Sartreanism to an American audience in the *New Republic* in 1945, continued to produce articles and teach classes on existentialism at the University of Chicago and other major universities. Maurice Natanson, a Yale professor and the first American philosopher to try to sort out Sartrean ontology in a book-length work, remembered the contribution of European philosophers to existentialist scholarship in America during these early years. Natanson studied at the New School for Social Research in New York and spoke fondly of the New School as "a kind of Garden of Eden" of people who understood existentialism and phenomenology. Natanson published *A Critique of Jean-Paul Sartre's Ontology* in 1951 and then went on to earn a second doctorate in sociology at the New School where European philosophers fanned his interest in Continental thought.[3]

Lack of translation in this period again favored American commentators who were fluent in French. Catherine Rau, an instructor in the Philosophy Department at the University of California, Berkeley, in the 1940s, studied at the Sorbonne from 1925 to 1938. Driven out of France by the onset of the war, she returned to America and earned her doctorate in philosophy at Berkeley. Finding Sartre's writing sprinkled with colloquialisms, Rau provided a necessary service to her colleagues by explaining difficult passages and producing critical essays. Sartre used "street French" liberally, Rau has recalled, and she believed one could not understand his subtleties without knowing the language intimately.[4]

The gradual increase in Sartrean scholarship by American philosophers also accelerated the legitimizing process. Now philosophers were more likely to be introduced to Sartre's doctrines by colleagues rather than by professors of literature or literary critics. Comments about the folly of paying attention to this new movement because it was "only literary"—while never completely disappearing—substantially diminished. The renewed flow of graduate students in philosophy to European universities in 1949 served in a small way to make more American philosophers aware of Sartreanism and thereby to increase its credibility. Arthur Danto, a member of the first group of Fulbright scholars to study philosophy in France after the war and later chair of the Columbia University philosophy department, felt the emotional tug of Sartre's ideas while in Paris. He did not believe at the time, however, that they merited serious consideration, for Sartreanism's association with bohemianism was too strong: "I was awfully young, and thoughts about hell being other people, or that we are what we do, seemed terribly interesting . . . [but] existentialism was by then pretty much part of the bohemian life of Paris and one took it in that way. I did not read very deeply."[5]

Danto followed the path of analytic philosophy but maintained some interest in Sartre. When asked to write a study of Sartre in the early 1970s, he agreed. After immersing himself in the French philosophy, Danto emerged with the realization that "I am in no sense an existentialist, but I am probably one of the rare analytic philosophers who on occasion thinks of certain things that Sartre got just right."[6] For Danto, then, an early interest was rekindled thirty years later.

Eugene Kaelin, a philosophy professor at Florida State University who later made Sartrean aesthetics his specialty, remembered his encounter with the French philosophy as a postwar Fulbright fellow in a more positive light: "For those of us who favored the European way, the philosophy was relevant to the philosophical concerns of the general populace having gone through a destruction of the established values of Western societies during the Second World War."[7] Kaelin also found existentialism useful as a tool of analysis in aesthetics and as a philosophy of mind and action that respected human choice.[8] Kaelin encountered some of the major figures in Continental thought at Bordeaux: Heidegger, Husserl, Sartre, and Maurice Merleau-Ponty. When he returned to America from a second trip to Bordeaux as a postdoctoral fellow, he made existentialism his focus. Philosophy students finishing graduate work abroad naturally had mixed opinions, but, at the minimum, contact with the Parisian intellectual environment expanded Americans' awareness of Sartre's ideas.

The internationalistic "one-world" spirit circulating in the philosophical community (as in American culture generally) after the war encouraged interest in Sartreanism as well. Some American philosophers, hoping that the reconciliation of opposing systems like materialism and idealism would help promote world peace, worked diligently in groups like UNESCO to achieve that end. Sartreanism attracted attention as philosophers strove to learn more about philosophical currents outside the Anglo-American milieu. One by-product of this globalism was the 1950 publication of *Philosophic Thought in France and the United States*.[9] Sponsored by UNESCO and edited by Marvin Farber, a leader of the American phenomenological movement at the University of Chicago, *Philosophic Thought in France and the United States* contained essays by both French and American philosophers that were devoted to explaining contemporary philosophical trends in the two countries.

The translation of other important works of Continental existentialism also benefited Sartrean scholarship in America; the appearance of Heidegger's *Existence and Being* in 1949 was a particular boon.[10] Now some of the deeper roots of Sartre's thought became more visible, and the unique characteristics of Sartreanism more distinguishable. Finally, the tempering of Sartre's initial faddishness in France and America helped to remove an obstacle that made it difficult for many American philosophers to take him seriously. Although Sartreanism had certainly not become a circumspect or quiet movement, at least it had reached the high-water mark of its notoriety and was becoming more similar to other philosophical currents in its ability to attract scholarly attention.

* * *

Fresh topics were interwoven with the original themes that surfaced in the earliest phase of Sartreanism's American encounter during this second stage. The publication of *The Emotions* and *The Psychology of the Imagination* naturally led to a new exploration of Sartre's interest in the function of the emotions and aesthetic theory. Another important subject was the growing realization of similarities between Sartrean thought and the philosophical currents that contoured the American milieu. But embedded in these new discoveries was the constant awareness of Sartreanism's opposition to the dominant empirical and analytic strains in America.

The 1948 translation of *The Emotions* showed philosophers unfamiliar with Sartre's early works that Sartre was deeply involved in the application of philosophical methodologies and insights to psychology. Sartre's intent in *The Emotions* was to criticize existing models of emotion and to offer a preliminary outline for a phenomenological psychology that would be based on an examination of essential structures of consciousness rather than on what Sartre perceived as an unintegrated collection of scientific facts. Sartre insisted that only a phenomenologically based theory could disclose the real significance of feelings. Other perspectives, he argued, were too positivisitic; they created images of emotions extrapolated from isolated, empirical findings that were falsely thought to be independent of the subjectivity of the theorist. A gathering of discrete facts, contended Sartre, did not add up to a true picture of emotion as an essential function of consciousness and a creative mode of apprehending the world. And although Sartre believed that rationalistic, instrumental apprehension was still the fundamental structure of consciousness, he made the emotional, inventive consciousness a much more important viewpoint than many philosophers did.[11]

Although the topic of emotion was new, old themes like Sartre's anti-empiricism quickly reappeared in American philosophers' responses. At the center of this disagreement over empirically based psychological interpretations of emotion was the issue of Sartre's epistemological foundation. Americans tended to take a strong stance: Disregard for empirical fact was unconscionable; knowledge could only be reached by empirical pathways. For Sartre, such a course led to scientific mystification.

Grene, who in 1947 published the first comparative essay on Sartre and Heidegger written by an American philosopher, was also one of the first to evaluate Sartre's model of emotion in detail. "Sartre's Theory of the Emotions," published in the *Yale French Studies* in 1948, was not widely read by her colleagues in philosophy because it appeared in a journal devoted to literary concerns, but it was significant because it showed the way in which particular philosophical experience, training, and temper could soften a negative evaluation of Sartreanism.[12]

Grene forthrightly disavowed Sartreanism in the late 1940s. Her essay on the emotions also revealed the American tendency to protest Sartre's lack of an "acceptable" empirical framework. At times she criticized Sartre's blanket opposition to science, but she was also skeptical of empiricism as it was narrowly construed. Grene's participation in Carnap's research seminar at the University of Chicago in 1937, where she acquired a powerful distaste for logical positivism rather than being drawn into the fold by Carnap, made her more inclined to share Sartre's view of empiricism as too positivistic. And although Grene had little sympathy for the German existentialism she studied as a graduate student in Europe, her familiarity with its intricacies made her less likely to view Sartreanism one-dimensionally and more capable of finding specific ideas worthy of merit.

If Grene's philosophical training made it easier for her to discern some useful directions in Sartre's work, so did her philosophical temper. Grene's willingness to praise the parts as being separate from the whole prevented her from completely rejecting Sartreanism. She acknowledged substantial nuggets of truth in the French philosophy and approved the blending of traditional psychology and an existential and phenomenological approach derived from experience; she also recognized the importance of an emotional apprehension of the world. Yet when Grene considered the tremendous significance Sartre gave to feelings as a dynamic existential structure of consciousness, she wavered: "There is always the suspicion, with Sartre's theories, that they are a bit too apt—or at least too clever, in a flashy way, to be quite true."[13]

* * *

The translation of *The Psychology of the Imagination* in 1948 and of *What Is Literature?* in 1949 directed American philosophers' attention to another new topic, Sartrean aesthetics.[14] These works came at an opportune time because interest in aesthetic theory in America was blossoming; growth in the field was rapid in the 1940s. The founding of the *Journal of Aesthetics and Art Criticism* and the organization of the American Society for Aesthetics in 1942, along with the proliferation of college courses and published works, all testified to a burgeoning concern. French and American philosophers had taken the lead in aesthetic theory.[15]

But within this new topic, the tried-and-true theme of antiempiricism bubbled up once again. Sartrean aesthetics met with opposition in the philosophical milieu of the United States because in America the currents of empiricism and naturalism had washed over aesthetics too. As Thomas Munro, a Rutgers philosophy professor and the editor of the *Journal of Aesthetics and Art Criticism,* observed in 1950: "We are the heirs of the long British tradition in the philosophy and psychology of art. It has been, on the whole, one of naturalism and empiricism."[16]

Sartre's *Psychology,* in stark contrast, presented a phenomenological analysis of the imagination as a particular mode of consciousness. His objective was to restore to this creative function the importance it had lost when psychologists ceased to believe in imagination as a discrete "mental faculty." Sartre presented imagination as a type of thought whose nature and laws were completely independent of sensation and perception. The imagination became a type of consciousness that grasped objects by direct intuition. And because imagination gave individuals the power to negate the world, Sartre maintained that it was an inexpungible source of human freedom. In one breath, Sartre equated the imagination with negativity because to imagine something was to negate the world and to insert a kind of nothingness, but he simultaneously insisted that imagination had a positive function because the ability to negate was a necessary condition for human freedom.[17]

For more than one American philosopher, the ambiguity of Sartre's negative and positive depiction of imagination amounted to an abuse of language; it was philosophical obscurantism! Hook raked Sartre over the coals of philosophical rigor in his 1948 review of *The Emotions* in the *New York Times*.[18] After criticizing Sartreanism for wandering too near the edge of "introspective psychology" and for being too derivative of German existentialism, Hook focused on Sartre's concept of nothingness as the weakest link. The emergence of human reality in nothingness, stressed Hook, can only happen through the existence of something. Sartre's positioning of the heart of reality—considered by Sartre to be the freedom of consciousness—in nothingness was, for Hook, the height of illogic and linguistic manipulation. Sartre's lack of semantic clarity was an issue that would continue to reverberate throughout the philosophical community in later years; many philosophers protested the ambiguity Sartre built into key categories such as "being" and "nothingness."

Hook was also suspicious of Sartre's inquiry into the nature of imagination because Sartre's conclusions seemed to be the result of a need to shore up the speculative tenets upon which the broader philosophical framework of existentialism depended. Sartre was not interested in gaining new knowledge about imagination, charged Hook, but merely in constructing a theory that would validate a priori beliefs. Hook observed that Sartre was "rather cavalier about negative evidence" and faulted him for an unwillingness to entertain the possibility that his philosophical tenets were open to question.[19] Here the strong-minded Hook confronted an equally resolute philosopher in Sartre, and in later years their disagreement would intensify.

Sartre's devotion to what Van Meter Ames, an aesthetician at the University of Cincinnati, labeled "a pragmatic theory of art" met with instant approval among some American philosophers. Although Ames was a very vocal opponent of Sartre's rejection of empiricism, and although Ames took the negative view in the first published debate in America over the ultimate philosophical value of Sartreanism, he did find some merit in Sartre's aesthetics. In "Existentialism and the Arts," an article published in the *Journal of Aesthetics and Art Criticism* in 1951, Ames likened Sartre's theory that writing should be a commitment to social change to the pragmatic view that people's needs, desires, and aversions propelled them to action. The choice of "pragmatic" to describe this idea pointed to an increasing attentiveness to congruities between American philosophical currents and Sartreanism. The concept of art as an action imbued with social responsibility—a medium to be developed in the interest of general social welfare—appealed to many philosophers in this era. Ames applauded Sartre's vision of art "as a creative activity in the service of freedom and control for a good life." In "The Aesthetic Views of Jean-Paul Sartre," an article published in the *Journal of Aesthetics and Art Criticism* in 1950, Rau, at the University of California, Berkeley, also praised Sartre for presenting art as an engine for democratic social progress.[20]

But however much the "pragmatic theory of art" appealed, these philosophers were dismayed by the absence of what they perceived as a sound empirical foundation for Sartre's aesthetics. How could Sartre support his position that literature was the expression of the need for social change, Rau asked, when his psychological assumptions were "not only capricious and sometimes even fantastic, but also vague and confused?" Ames agreed with Rau and extended the discussion of Sartre's antiempiricism when he wondered why Sartre was unable to see that science as well as art could also be used as a force for social progress.[21]

Rau and Ames approached Sartre's aesthetic theories from the vantage point of philosophers primarily concerned with making aesthetics compatible with an empirical methodology. Barrett, a philosopher at New York University whose interest in literature found an outlet through his activities as an editor of the *Partisan Review,* evaluated Sartre's concept of engaged literature as a political stance. Barrett agreed with the idea of politically responsible literature insofar as it represented a reintegration of art and life, but he adamantly opposed Sartre's design to subjugate literature to suit socialist ends. For Barrett, such an aesthetic was wrongheaded. Literature should not be limited by any political theory because that would result in second-rate writing— in this case, literature watered down to appeal to the greatest number of people and to propel them toward a socialist revolution.[22] In sum, the Sartrean vision of aesthetic theory as a forceful agent in the march toward social progress struck some responsive chords among American philosophers, but the divergence of Sartrean doctrines from the naturalistic and empirical tendencies of American aesthetics, as well as their political ramifications, ultimately limited Sartreanism's appeal.

* * *

The similarity between Sartreanism and dominant currents in American philosophy was another topic that received more attention now. Of course some awareness of likenesses had already surfaced in the earliest commentary; Sellars, a founder of the American school of critical realism whose support of democratic socialism encouraged him to keep abreast of Sartrean thought, reflected in 1947 that Sartre's discussion of human existence reminded him of Ralph Waldo Emerson's ideas on the self: "Each is what he makes himself. There is a touch of Emersonianism in it but less tranquil in tone." Philosophers expanded discussions of resemblances in the late 1940s and early 1950s. In vein, Rau also discovered Sartre's "Emersonianism" in 1949, and emphasized the French philosopher's insistence on action and courage in the face of defeat as well as the impossibility of making a priori moral choices. Rau underscored these similarities when she concluded in "The Ethical Theory of Jean-Paul Sartre," an article published in the *Journal of Philosophy* in 1949, "Existentialism is a fine sermon on self-reliance."[23]

Grene compiled a long list of parallelisms between existentialism and dominant American perspectives in philosophy in *Dreadful Freedom: A Critique of Existentialism,* the first book-length study of Sartreanism as a philosophical totality by an American philosopher. Both existentialism and the powerful American currents of empiricism and analysis, Grene argued, were offspring of the rebellion against Hegelian idealism in particular and metaphysical system building in general. She also noted the affinity between pragmatic and existentialist epistemology which subordinated knowing to doing. Grene also found similarities in Sartre's and John Dewey's accounts of the genesis of philosophical systems, a connection that Hook, Dewey's disciple and heir, would also note at a later date. Both stressed the social function of philosophical speculation—the extent to which philosophy stabilized the norms used by a powerful social group to maintain its control. Grene remarked on both individuals' desire to turn philosophy toward the future and to use it to usher in progressive social change. Although Dewey was by far the more careful philosopher in a technical sense, and although Sartre and Dewey were opposed on the basic issues of epistemology and value theory, there was a marked similarity in their fervent interest in actively using philosophy to solve social problems.[24]

Growing familiarity with Sartre's thought, helped along by newly translated works and the increase in commentary, made it easier for American philosophers to recognize commonalities as well as differences in the dominant strains in philosophical environments. The new attention paid to likenesses represented an evolution too. Differences stood out when new ideas were first confronted, but in the course of time, increased knowledge and reflection brought recognition of similarities with established strains of thought.

Some American philosophers stressed the possibility of rapprochement—the development of a productive relationship between empirically and analytically oriented American philosophy and Continental existentialism. Consideration of both perspectives from the vantage point of a shared criterion rather than from first principles, purposes, and methods enabled McKeon, the Spinoza scholar at the University of Chicago, to stress likenesses. McKeon was another philosopher whose study at the Sorbonne in the 1920s increased his fluency in French. He was an outspoken member of the U.S. delegation to the General Conference of UNESCO from 1946 to 1949, and he firmly believed that the philosophical melding of divergent systems would bring world peace. This point of view encouraged McKeon to see the main currents of French and American thought as moving along parallel lines, and he presented this argument in "An American Reaction to the Present Situation in French Philosophy," an essay published in *Philosophic Thought in France and the United States*.[25]

McKeon, who also served as president of the Central Division of the American Philosophical Association in 1952, contended that the shared criterion of existence as a philosophical touchstone gave empirically oriented philosophies and existentialism a common base on which to build a dialogue. This criterion was evident in American philosophy, he argued, if differences in approach, goals, and first principles did not obscure it. American philosophers sought the existential in "relations" rather than in consciousness, located experience in events rather than mental acts, and analyzed experience in terms of "problems and solutions" rather than "immanence and transcendence." In America the search for the organic whole tended to move from the situation to the society or universe, McKeon observed, instead of from the ego to the absolute or nothingness.[26]

McKeon concluded that in both France and America a similar quest was under way for the organic, the existential, and the circumstantial. Although he was very much aware of the differences between the dominant American and French movements, he argued that the shared concept of the existential provided a pathway for future philosophical communication. But because of substantial disagreements over methodology and goals, the road toward philosophical understanding was full of obstacles.

McKeon was not alone in his vision of increased exchange between American philosophers and French existentialists. The possibility of more felicitous communication was suggested by others in the late 1940s and early 1950s. The partial reconciliation that began to be visible in this period had two levels: One was an awareness that science-based philosophies and existentialism could be complementary, the other was an increasing recognition of changes in the philosophical doctrines of both strains of thought that brought them closer together. At a meeting of the Eastern Division of the American Philosophical Association in December 1949, John Smith, then a young professor at Barnard who later became a distinguished scholar of the history of American philosophy and the philosophy of religion at Yale, read a paper entitled "Is Existence a Valid Philosophical Concept?"[27] Here Smith scrutinized the competing views of existence in science-based and existentialist thought and decided it was philosophically necessary to incorporate elements of both perspectives to arrive at a satisfactory concept of existence.

Smith pointed out that the idea of existence presented by existentialists like Sartre was too limited because existence was reduced to its human component. What was the value of restricting one's vision to human existence when the world was the setting for many other existential experiences? Conversely, Smith also found the American "empirical" concept too narrow precisely because it neglected the human level. He was disturbed by what he perceived as a growing inclination among colleagues to forgo inquiries directly relevant to human activity. Smith called instead for an integrative philosophy where thinking did not occur in a rarefied world beyond the one in which the individual existed; instead, philosophers would be cognizant of conditions imposed both by the physical environment and by their own human interests. The nonhuman and human planes, Smith observed, were necessarily inseparable: "It is only at the level of human existence that the problem of interpreting the whole of existence arises."[28]

The method that Smith used to establish his argument documented this interdependency: He relied on principles and methods from both traditions to prove his point. In the language of analytic philosophy, Smith asked, "Is there a concept of existence?" and "Is the question 'Why does anything exist' meaningful?" Satisfied that both questions could be answered positively without compromising the strengths in the methodology of philosophical analysis, Smith believed that the existentialist focus on human consciousness could be profitably incorporated into a discourse that also paid attention to rigorous linguistic guidelines. When American philosophers adopted a more inclusive view of existence, Smith argued, the method of inquiry should be compatible with the analytic tradition. The philosopher was to discover by analysis "the precise formulation of the basic structure in which all existents participate" and was to interpret experience by providing "an intelligible account of all levels of existence."[29]

Smith's paper represented an early effort to spell out precisely how American philosophers could fill in the gaps in French existentialism that they spotted from the beginning. By embracing an existentialist principle but by retaining an empirical concept of existence and analytic methodology, Smith laid important groundwork for a possible integration. He also expressed a growing sentiment among American philosophers that human existence had been given short shrift by the empiricists, and this feeling naturally encouraged a more thoughtful consideration of Sartreanism.

Philip Rice, the chair of the philosophy department at Kenyon College, echoed the theme that both Anglo-American and existentialist traditions could be viewed as complementary. Rice tried to make Kenyon a gathering place for scholars interested in existentialism until his untimely death in 1956. Deeply interested in aesthetics and the interconnections between literature and philosophy, Rice chided his American colleagues for immersing themselves in overspecialized pursuits, and Continental philosophers for philosophizing in too grand a fashion. Rice observed in "The Children of Narcissus: Some Themes of French Speculation," an article published in the *Kenyon Review* in 1950: "The French philosophers have at least been seeking wisdom, whereas our own younger men have been seeking merely clarity."[30] The Kenyon professor saw the philosophical profit in combining these approaches.

Other philosophers discussed the relationship between existentialism and American philosophy on another level: They pointed to recent signs of convergence. Mary Coolidge, an influential philosophy professor (and former dean) at Wellesley College, was one of the first to suggest such a trend in "Some Vicissitudes of the Once-Born and of the Twice-Born Man," an article published in *Philosophy and Phenomenological Research* in 1950.[31] As part of her doctoral program, Coolidge traveled to Germany to study Continental thought, and her subsequent specialization in German philosophy and aesthetics made her particularly attentive to Sartreanism.

Coolidge argued that the dominant American philosophical tendency—one she labeled "empirical naturalism"—appealed to "once-born individuals while atheistic existentialisms like Sartreanism appealed to the 'twice-born.'" Coolidge borrowed the categories of "once-born" and "twice-born" from William James who had borrowed them from Cardinal John Henry Newman. The fundamental difference between the two approaches, according to Coolidge, was that the once-born perspective was optimistic. The twice-born philosophy, by contrast, emphasized the existence of evil; it was essentially a philosophy of despair.[32] Once-born, empirical, and naturalistic strains of thought also viewed individuals in very different ways from those of twice-born, existentialist doctrines. These philosophies assessed the individual externally. The model of the person was derived by collecting scientific data and establishing a norm; the "individual" who emerged was not really an individual at all. Twice-born, or existentialist, perspectives, Coolidge observed, went the other way around. Their image of personhood was derived by studying the individual from the inside; subjectivity rather than objectivity was the starting point. The model that grew out of this approach stressed the uniqueness of selfhood and rejected scientific norms.

The philosophical shift that Coolidge perceived was a gradual recognition on the part of "once-born" philosophies of the reality of evil in the modern world and increasing awareness of human subjectivity and experience as a source of knowledge and value formation. Coincidentally, Coolidge saw in Sartreanism a movement toward a greater optimism—a belief in the possibility of human salvation in a godless world. Sartrean salvation was attained through personal honesty, activity in the social and political world, and acknowledgment of personal freedom and the freedom of others.[33]

The context of Coolidge's thoughtful description of convergence was telling because the entire analysis was conceived within a Jamesian model. Indeed, she insisted, the patron saint of pragmatism blessed the American and French rapprochement: "James would surely have been interested in watching once-born American individuals facing the brute facts of the modern world. . . . And he could thus hardly have failed to regard sympathetically the struggle of twice-born European individuals to preserve man's freedom, and to enable him to pass both through, and beyond, despair."[34]

Coolidge's essay marked a turning point in the evolution of Sartreanism in the United States. Hers was the first to cast a discussion of Sartre totally within the structure of an American philosopher's thought. Certainly, others had noted strong affinities between Sartre and the various strains of pragmatism, but Coolidge went a step beyond by analyzing Sartreanism wholly within a Jamesian framework. Because James was considered such a quintessentially American philosopher, Coolidge's analysis constituted a significant step toward the Americanization of Sartre—a never completed process that consisted of selecting out particular doctrines that had national resonance rather than the wholesale adoption of Sartre's principles and methods.

Coolidge's awareness of the movement of the American philosophical community away from the presumption of goodness and benign progress within the world was prophetic, too, for the continuation of this shift would help provide a more welcoming environment for Sartre. The significance of Coolidge's gesture, however, was more suggestive than definitive in 1950. American philosophers certainly did not all follow in Coolidge's footsteps, but her method did mark a growing consciousness of similarities between Sartreanism and particular threads in American philosophy; Sartreanism was becoming less alien.

The evolution of Sartreanism, then, advanced along another important front in the late 1940s and early 1950s. Not only did it gain credibility as a legitimate philosophical inquiry, but some began to suggest the possibility of integration. Grene discussed a long list of similarities and dissimilarities between American and French philosophical currents. Smith and Rice brought to the philosophical foreground the methodological necessity of incorporating particular existentialist concepts into the American milieu. Coolidge and McKeon took the further step of emphasizing areas in which dominant strains in both American and French philosophy were compatible. These philosophers helped open the door to a philosophical dialogue.

* * *

The criticisms that surfaced when Sartreanism was first introduced in America were interwoven with expressions of interest; now they merged with the new topics of the nature of human emotion, aesthetic theory, and a possible rapprochement between Anglo-American and existentialist philosophy. Faultfinding included skepticism regarding Sartre's ties to bohemianism, the French Resistance movement, and Marxism. Other motifs of a more properly philosophic character continued too; Sartre's antiempiricism and opposition to philosophical analysis were the loudest recurring complaints.

Sartreanism's association with intellectual bohemianism still raised a few eyebrows in the late 1940s and early 1950s. Barnes, who played such an important role in spreading Sartreanism in America by virtue of her translations and informed commentary, remembered that some colleagues continued to believe that Sartrean doctrines were the frothy by-products of café society and a lunatic fringe. Barnes found this view limited to those who in reality knew very little about Sartreanism: "They looked on it with the sublime contempt possible only for total ignorance."[35] Grene offered a terse reminder of some philosophers' unfamiliarity and hostility during the annual meeting of the Western Division of the American Philosophical Association in 1949. Grene presented a lecture on Sartre, and at its close a member of the audience asked, "Is this man [Sartre] a fool?" "No," Grene replied wittily, "he is a Frenchman."[36] But although philosophers with any knowledge of existentialism did not make such facile judgments, the stigma of bohemianism still tainted Sartreanism. The connection between the French philosophy and intellectual bohemianism, however, did become less damning during the second phase of contact; greater familiarity with the range and depth of Sartre's inquiries eventually began to temper the negative association.

Kraushaar, the Smith College professor who went to the extreme of equating the philosophical impact of Sartreanism with the negative consequence of handing a baboon a machine gun when he reviewed *Existentialism* in 1947, noted then that "even the existentialists cannot escape history."[37] This idea that the universality of Sartrean principles was vitiated by its connection with the French Resistance endured. As had been true in the first phase of contact, the majority of American philosophers now clearly recognized that Sartreanism was not solely a philosophical manifestation of that unique event, but they did believe that the Resistance had deeply imprinted Sartre's thought. In the second phase of contact, philosophers looked more closely at the charges that Sartrean ethics and ontology lacked universality.

Grene was one philosopher who perceived strengths within the weaknesses; Sartreanism's connection with the Resistance, she felt, limited the generality of some of its principles, but she also believed the philosophy offered some unimpugnable moral advice. Grene was forthright about the discrepancy between Sartre's fundamental perspective of the individual as an alienated being and his rather sudden declaration of the possibility of a social morality at the end of *L'Être et le néant*. Sartre's transition to a social ethic in which the individual acted in a manner that preserved universal freedoms, observed Grene, was the result of the searing experience of the German occupation. During the occupation it was true that individual acts could determine the liberty of many people, but that situation, and others like it, were exceptional. Grene was disturbed by the absence of a philosophical link that logically bound Sartre's image of the self to his new social ethics. But even though the French philosopher failed to expand an ethic most applicable in the unique situation of war into a universal rule, the concept still held some good moral advice.[38]

John Smith at Barnard College was more troubled by the theoretical inconsistency between what he believed was Sartre's depiction of a privatized self and the declaration that individual actions had universal implications. Smith later turned Sartre's own rhetoric against him and labeled Sartre's efforts to establish a social ethics an "exercise in bad faith." The Barnard philosophy professor felt that Sartre had misled people by suggesting in *Existentialism* that he had always supported the Kantian universality principle instead of acknowledging what Smith believed: that Sartre had adopted it to counter Marxist critics who charged him with advocating an unqualified individualism. Reflecting on his assessment of Sartrean ethics thirty years later, Smith still maintained that "there was no way in which his [Sartre's] individuals could form any community."[39]

The validity of Sartre's social ethics emerged as an important issue during these years. Many American philosophers agreed with Grene and Smith that Sartre's postwar social ethics was logically inconsistent with the predominant view of the individual in Sartre's earlier work. Philosophers varied in their response to the problem. Some acknowledged the difficulty but still found Sartre's ethics valuable; others felt that the lack of an adequate logical framework nullified the worth of specific ethical principles.

Herbert Marcuse examined the relationship of Sartreanism to the French Resistance from a slightly different perspective: ontology. Marcuse, a German-Jewish Marxist philosopher who immigrated to the

United States in 1934 as a refugee from Nazism, discussed Sartre's ontology in "Remarks on Jean-Paul Sartre's *L'Être et le néant,*" a 1948 essay published in *Philosophy and Phenomenological Research.* Marcuse argued that Sartre hypostatized the irrational nature of a particular historical situation—the Resistance—into an ontology: "The experience of the absurdity of the world, of man's failure and frustration appears as the experience of his ontological condition."[40]

Sartre's expansion of a unique circumstance into a universal ontological state, Marcuse contended, turned his philosophy into a bourgeois idealism. The fallacious identity of ontology and historical subjectivity prevented the successful development of a philosophy of concrete existence. But in spite of this fundamental objection, Marcuse, like others, found some ethical merit in Sartre. Ironically, he concluded by praising Sartre for teaching people to abandon utopian dreams and to plant themselves on the firm ground of reality. In short, Sartre's ties to the particular historical situation of the French Resistance remained problematic for philosophers on both ethical and ontological grounds. Philosophers' ability to find important moral insights and lines of inquiry in Sartre's thought depended partly on their willingness to forgive Sartre for generalizing specific conditions into universal states. And some philosophers were very much affected by the aura of the Resistance and Sartre's image as a Resistance hero. The mistaken perception that persisted in the aftermath of the war that Sartre put himself at risk by opposing the occupation made philosophers such as Grene feel that there was incomplete justification in criticizing his ethics; most philosophers, Grene then believed, had not put themselves on the same line.[41]

Because American philosophers naturally made philosophical issues the focal point of the criticisms that appeared in their journals, views on Sartre's activities in the tumultuous world of postwar French politics often were not publicly discussed; many, however, were aware of Sartre's attempt to transcend democracy as it was practiced in the United States and to transcend communism as it was practiced in the Soviet Union and to find "a third way." Those who read *Existentialism* recognized the partisan arguments that Sartre was involved in because of the book's inclusion of a debate with Marxist opponents; others no doubt followed the coverage of Sartre's political strategizing in newspapers and magazines. From the beginning, some Americans were put off by what they perceived as Sartre's overzealous and naive adherence to Marxism. Grene remembered: "I had been asked to write about existentialism: holding in my hand a copy of [Merleau-Ponty's] *La Phénoménologie de la Perception,* I said to myself, 'Another of Sartre's Marxists—No!'"[42]

The few American thinkers who did discuss Sartre's politics in print in the late 1940s and early 1950s considered it as a theoretical political philosophy and as an embattled political entity. These philosophers typically agreed with Marxists who dismissed as unsuccessful Sartre's attempts to transcend an individualistic form of liberalism but, unlike the Marxists, they believed Sartre's emphasis on the individual was a positive and not a liability. Stuart Brown, a philosophy professor at Cornell whose later interests included the philosophical ramifications of science and technology, praised Sartre for trying to salvage the individualistic element in liberalism in "The Atheistic Existentialism of Jean-Paul Sartre," an article published in the *Philosophical Review* in 1948.[43] Brown was another philosopher who found Sartreanism compelling in the late 1940s because it spoke directly to the experience of moral uncertainty in the midst of World War II. He was one of the handful of American philosophers who were introduced to Sartreanism during the war, and he tried to contact Sartre while serving in the U.S. Army Signal Corps in Europe between 1943 and 1946. Brown was so interested in Sartre's effort to construct a philosophical edifice that would account for the ethical absurdity of war that when he was awarded a Rockefeller Post-War Fellowship in 1947 he spent the year trying to achieve some understanding of existentialism and come to terms with it.

Sartre's lasting influence on Stuart Brown's philosophical point of view was mild in the long run; in later years he described his own ethical theory as "primarily Aristotelian with modifications suggested by W. D. Ross."[44] But Brown's investigation of Sartrean morality in the late 1940s was telling. It suggested the appeal of a philosophy that tried to sort out the issues of freedom and responsibility that World War II so dramatically brought into focus. "The Atheistic Existentialism of Jean-Paul Sartre" was the fruit of Brown's year of reflection, and here the Cornell philosopher stressed the merit of Sartre's effort to preserve a linkage between freedom and responsibility in ethical theory: "In his [Sartre's] emphasis upon individual freedom, together with individual responsibility, he preserved what he thinks possible out of the tradition of liberalism."[45]

Marxist foes attacked Sartre as a dangerous bourgeois liberal on the nontheoretical political plane, while American liberals often felt that he was too uncritical of the Communist Party. The controversy over Sartre's politics revealed ambiguities in the concept of liberalism, and the perspectives of two American philosophers—Hook and Barrett— clearly outlined these fissures in the liberal philosophical community. Both Hook and Barrett believed that Sartre was too accepting of the totalitarian aspects of the Communist Party and that his political solutions were naive and ineffective. Hook, however, insisted that liberals should reject Sartre because he was too conciliatory to Stalinism, while Barrett argued that they should embrace Sartre precisely because he was at least criticizing Stalinist-driven communism.

The difference in Hook's and Barrett's view of Sartrean politics was a matter of degree rather than kind. The split that emerged in American liberalism in the 1930s that turned some radicals into staunch opponents of Stalinism and made others into apologists left both Hook and Barrett on the anti-Stalinist side of that divide in later years. But they still disagreed on the sufficiency of Sartre's critique of the Soviet dictator. Hook was particularly hostile to Sartre's rather quixotic fellow traveling and increased opposition to American foreign policy in western Europe in the late 1940s.

Hook and Sartre locked horns over the motives underlying the Marshall Plan and the Atlantic Charter at the International Day of Resistance against War and Fascism on 30 April 1949 in Paris. Hook had been invited by David Rousset, the leader of the anti-Stalinist socialist Rassemblement Démocratique Révolutionnaire (RDR), to address the crowd gathered for the event. Earlier, Rousset had convinced a dubious Sartre to join the RDR; Sartre was very skeptical of Rousset's ties to the existing political power structure in America and stalwart anticommunists like Hook. Hook described himself in his speech on the International Day of Resistance as a socialist, but one opposed to any socialism or communism that sought power through terrorism or coercion. He proceeded to defend both the Marshall Plan and the Atlantic Pact on the grounds that they were essentially ameliorative efforts designed to further peace and economic recovery.[46]

Sartre followed Hook's address with an announcement of his resignation from the RDR. The group's invitation to Hook and Hook's support of American foreign policy in Europe were the final straws that led to Sartre's withdrawal from the American-subsidized RDR. Sartre also took this opportunity to make clear his opposition to what he viewed as the imperialistic overtones of the Marshall Plan and the Atlantic Pact. These protests intensified Hook's perception of Sartre as a defender of the Communist Party and a political naïf. Hook decided that "it was not as a Marxist that Sartre's thought was mischievous but as an obsessive anti-anti-communist."[47]

Barrett also felt that Sartre was not critical enough of the Communists: "In general, it can be said of Sartre that he has come to Marxism too late, that he has not lived through it and beyond it, so that he still sees political and cultural realities under the too drastic Marxist simplifications."[48] But Barrett gave Sartre credit for the anti-Stalinist stances he did take, while Hook stressed his pro-Communist actions at a time when the French philosopher was wobbling on the political fence between democratic socialism and the Stalinist-dominated Communist Party.

Barrett and Hook were exceptional in this period because the attention they paid to Sartrean politics far exceeded that of the majority of their colleagues. What was obvious in this critique by American philosophers was its essential difference from that of Communist Party faultfinders. Those foes claimed that Sartre was not supportive enough of the party, while American philosophers typically found him too uncritical. It was, of course, difficult for either group simultaneously to praise Sartre for trying to preserve the virtues of both democratic socialism and a non-Stalinist Communist Party, the dual objective the French philosopher had set for himself. Among Americans, then, a political fault line began to emerge. As time wore on, it became clear that philosophers like Barrett, who appreciated the elements of antitotalitarianism in existentialism, were more inclined to give it a sympathetic reading, while those who did not found dismissal easier. As the Cold War deepened, Sartre's increasingly critical view of U.S. foreign policy had a more negative impact on the philosophical community in the second stage of contact.

Opposition to Sartre's antiempiricism and antianalytic stance was another enduring motif, and now it emerged as a central concern in the discussion that served as a rite of passage. The first heated debate over the philosophical merit of Sartrean thought published in America got under way in the *Journal of Philosophy* in 1950. The participants were Ames, Natanson, and John Yolton. The debate began with the publication of Ames's "Fetishism in the Existentialism of Jean-Paul Sartre," an essay published in July 1950, whose patronizing tone clearly conveyed Ames's belief that Sartre was irrationally devoted to wrongheaded principles.[49] Natanson, author of the first book-length critique of Sartrean ontology by an American philosopher, challenged Ames's views. Yolton, then a Fulbright fellow at Oxford University and a Locke scholar who taught at Princeton in the mid-1950s, attempted to mediate the debate.

The issue of greatest importance in this exchange was the status of metaphysical explanation. Arguments about the significance of Sartrean thought in the late 1940s and early 1950s became part of the ongoing emotional debate among American philosophers over the value of traditional, rationalistic metaphysical methodologies. Traditional metaphysics, in which a deductive system rested on a priori maxims, had many foes. It was challenged by social scientists who pointed out that such systems reflected the conditions and needs of the culture from which they originated; psychologists in particular questioned the idea that reason was unaffected by basic human desires. Logical positivists in philosophy led the attack by protesting the lack of empirical meaning in metaphysics, and naturalists and analytic philosophers followed suit.[50]

Existentialists challenged metaphysics in the grand tradition too. Sartre vehemently opposed any speculative system that conceptualized reality in rationalistic terms. He tried to supplant traditional metaphysics with phenomenological ontology and hoped to replace the abstraction of speculative thought with the concreteness of phenomenological intuition.[51] The irony of the situation was that although Sartre considered himself an opponent of rational metaphysics, many of his critics accused him of continuing in that vein.[52]

The underlying theme in this debate over the status of metaphysical inquiry was a criticism of existentialism that had attached itself when Sartreanism was first introduced to America: antiempiricism and antianalysis. Sartre was accused of offering a metaphysics that rested on principles devoid of empirical or analytical justification. Ames argued that Sartre turned such key concepts as *existence, being, nothingness, freedom,* and *responsibility* into noun substantives that did not represent realities; by philosophical sleight of hand and the emotional use of language, Sartre created an extremely irrational world. Ames, however, did give Sartre credit for great skill in manipulating words like "freedom" that carried a high emotional charge in the aftermath of the war.

He noted how Sartre tailored his concept of freedom to intensify the ability of the individual to at least resist when all other freedoms were eliminated: "Even a philosophically seasoned person may be impressed, and should be if he has any appreciation of the terrifying experience of mankind in recent years."[53]

Essentially, Ames's philosophic complaint was that Sartre opposed the interrelated traditions of empiricism and linguistic analysis. "The sciences," said Ames sternly, "begin with experience and its problems, and so does philosophy when it makes sense." For Ames, Sartre's formulation of key terms as noun substantives having actual existence was an unconscionable violation of the canons of linguistic analysis. The use of fundamental concepts in such a manner, he declared, made "an absurd world because it is made of absurd words."[54]

Round two of the debate got under way with Natanson's rebuttal, "Sartre's Fetishism: A Reply to Van Meter Ames," published in the *Journal of Philosophy* in February 1951. Natanson, an expert on Sartrean ontology, maintained that Ames never confronted the central philosophical problem in *L'Être et le néant* or its historical roots. The difficulty was to explain "being" by way of a phenomenological method, Natanson argued. Natanson politely implied that Ames failed to consider Sartreanism in such a context because Ames was largely ignorant of the history of existentialist and phenomenological thought: "[I]t is impossible to understand Sartre's position without recognizing the fact that his is a radical ontology which attempts to explicate Being via an analysis of man's Being . . . historically associated with Kierkegaard, Hegel, Dilthey, Scheler, Husserl and Heidegger."[55] Natanson, in essence, spoke out against the lingering tendency among some philosophers to dismiss Sartre's ideas on the basis of a superficial reading or even no reading at all.

Natanson also vigorously challenged Ames's conclusion that Sartre divorced the individual from real human experience by creating fetishes that hypostatized human events. This criticism, he argued, merely revealed Ames's lack of understanding of the kind of philosophizing Sartre attempted. The whole point of Sartre's position was that a phenomenological analysis of individual being was the only form in which the new type of philosophical questioning that sought to include individual experience could occur; the discussion of human existence simply could not be reduced to the problem: Is existence a predicate? Natanson opposed the inclination in American philosophy to find little of value in Sartreanism because it violated largely unquestioned empirical and analytic canons.

Natanson staunchly maintained that human existence could not be fully explained in any language that would establish an empirical meaning criterion; the explanation could only be found in the complex dialectical relationship between the *en-soi* and the *pour-soi,* that elaborate intertwining of freedom, choice, negation, and situation. But Natanson's interest in Sartre's approach did not blind him to its defects. He questioned Sartre's modification of Husserlian methods and his attempted use of phenomenology to rescue metaphysics from the oblivion to which some philosophers wished to send it.[56]

Round three of the debate began with a crisp reply from Ames. The University of Cincinnati professor would not budge. Sartre's misuse of concepts, insisted Ames, "is so wanton—that the burden of proof is on a defender of Sartre to show that his use of terms is significant, instead of asking a critic to wander further in a dialectic without a thread of logic." Ames concluded that there was not enough shared agreement on the use of language to even sustain a discussion; his colleague accepted language that did not have empirical meaning and a dialectic that depended on mood and metaphor. Finally, Ames added a protest against Sartrean pessimism: "If we seek the irrational, the momentous, and passionate, especially in these dark days, we may as well build on love and beauty as on loneliness and dread."[57] Barrett's earlier prediction that Sarteanism was simply too bleak for American sensibilities was confirmed in Ames.

The last round was Yolton's attempted mediation in "The Metaphysic of *En-soi* and *Pour-soi.*" Yolton objected to Ames's position because Ames gave metaphysics too narrow a range by insisting that propositions had to conform to empirical demands for verifiable statements. He also protested American philosophers' tendency to reject Sartreanism on the basis of its gloomy overtones. Yolton sensed, as Barrett had, that the optimistic, "once-born" perspective of many American philosophers prompted negative reactions that colored their professional evaluation of its doctrines.[58]

Yolton praised Natanson for supporting the position that metaphysics need not meet empirical and analytic requirements, but noted that Natanson's argument was "too imbued with the language of Sartreanism to show that meaning and significance do attach to Sartre's still untranslated *L'Etre.*"[59] Seeking to explain Sartre's contribution in terms that Anglo-American philosophers could understand and possibly appreciate, Yolton argued that Sartre's chief contribution lay in his use of a phenomenological framework to explore the relation between subject and object and describe that relationship in terms of appearances: Reality was what appeared as present to observers.

Yolton could not bridge the distance between the two very different currents of thought. If Ames would allow the validity of a phenomenological perspective, Yolton argued, he would see that Sartre's concepts were not empty abstractions but real entities because people had experiences very similar to what Sartre described in such terms as "being-in-itself" or "being-for-itself." But Ames simply did not care whether he did or did not put Sartrean thought in a phenomenological structure, because he steadfastly believed that such a framework could never uncover truths about human existence. Unsurprisingly, the debate ended in an impasse. Neither Ames nor Natanson was able to convince the other to change his mind, and Yolton's effort to resolve the differences was unsuccessful too. Rice, the chair of the Philosophy Department at Kenyon College and a strong supporter of existentialism, described the opposing methodologies perfectly:

> The French thinkers accordingly indulge freely in a priori metaphysical constructions, without constraint from the semantic self-questionings and methodological hesitations that beset their American colleagues. This license saves the French philosophers from the myopia and speculative paralysis that too often inhibits contemporary Anglo-Saxon philosophy; it also renders a great deal of their writing either thinly rhetorical or tenuously dialectic.[60]

The 1950–51 debate was also revealing in other ways. It substantiated the commonsensical hypothesis that philosophers such as Natanson who were well schooled in Continental existentialism were more inclined to view Sartrean thought with greater understanding and sympathy; they were more accustomed to convoluted terminology and more intimately acquainted with the philosophical investigations of consciousness upon which Sartre built. The debate was significant not only because of the entrenched philosophical positions it revealed but because of the attempted mediation it called forth. Yolton's failed mission was of a piece with similar efforts made in this period. Growing familiarity with Sartrean thought made it easier for critics to sort out its strengths and weaknesses and to suggest ways of increasing communication between different idioms and approaches. But the gap between empirically and analytically oriented thinkers and those with existentialist and phenomenological perspectives would not be easily closed; a characteristic of this second stage of contact was the coexistence of the opposing impulse to cast out a philosophy that forthrightly contradicted "scientific" canons.

* * *

From the beginning, American philosophers found principles in Sartreanism that they could agree with, and in this second stage of response, such sympathetic resonances endured. Above all else, philosophers applauded Sartre's emphasis on individual freedom, personal responsibility, and authenticity. Approval, however, was often limited by the frequently repeated statement that although Sartre provided some fragments of valuable moral advice, he lacked a sound philosophical structure. Francis Randall remembered the attitude of his father, John Randall, and other naturalists at Columbia: "French existentialism was much sniffed at by philosophers who sympathized with the concerns but couldn't swallow what they saw as the naive philosophical approach."[61]

American thinkers recognized that France in particular needed a philosophy that stressed individual liberty and responsibility in order to rebuild a demoralized country. And many agreed that a doctrine with such an emphasis would also help shore up the more generalized war-induced fractures in liberalism and democracy throughout the world. Individual freedom, personal responsibility, and authenticity were interlocking concepts in Sartrean morality. Freedom implied responsibility and authenticity and was the state of recognizing both. Sartre argued that the key characteristic of the human condition was freedom—the ability to make a choice. As formulated in the 1940s and early 1950s, Sartrean freedom was a radical liberty. Although Sartre readily acknowledged that there was no such thing as absolute freedom because liberty was always affected by environmental forces, he contended that some degree of choice, however minute, remained within every situation. Because choice was an inalienable ingredient in human existence, individuals experienced "dread before nothingness." They were aware of their freedom to create values in a world in which preexisting standards were not set by supernatural beings or a rational order.

Responsibility followed on the heels of freedom. If people created their own values and could not look to religion, reason, or science for standards, they had to acknowledge personal responsibility for moral choices. To be "authentic" was to accept choice and responsibility. The process of becoming authentic was one of demystification, according to Sartre. The individual had to quit pretending that values emerged from anywhere other than the self. To fail to reach this realization was to live an inauthentic existence in "bad faith."[62]

What was it about the way that Sartre formulated his morality that American philosophers found particularly valuable? His consideration of personal freedom in a concrete, human situation rather than in an abstract, nonhuman framework attracted them, even as they complained about the absence of a logical structure. Sartreanism's main contribution, decided Grene, was precisely its correction of philosophies that found values emerging from factors largely independent of human choice: "It is the attempt to show the genesis of human values from the core of humanity that makes some of Sartre's ethical analysis—if not valid, at least terribly interesting."[63] The drift of American philosophy away from a priori ethical values meant that Sartre's central moral premise would find resonance in the United States. Even though philosophers might not be thoroughgoing ethical relativists themselves, they acknowledged that the moral ambiguity of Sartre's universe mirrored the situation in which many people in mid–twentieth-century Western society found themselves.

The Sartrean slogan "existence precedes essence" included the idea of the individual's freedom to choose values. Philosophers believed that this concept had wide appeal in an age when it was difficult to defend one ethical stance against others. The spread of ethical relativism meant that Sartre's principle of individual choice was one moral standard that could survive in a relativistic world. American philosophers also found merit in Sartre's conviction that individual liberty implied individual responsibility. Stuart Brown at Cornell University called Sartre a good "propagandist" for taking the important step of "urging upon each man the responsibility for creating conditions in which Man may again have dignity in his own eyes."[64]

Sartre's concept of authenticity began to have greater meaning as well in the late 1940s and 1950s. Philosophers now clearly distinguished Sartre's concept from that of the German existentialists. While Jaspers and Heidegger made authenticity a state achieved upon recognition of impending death, Sartre argued that authenticity was the result of awareness of individual freedom to create values. Articles that high-lighted this concept of authenticity began to appear in the philosophical literature.[65] For the first time, this idea was singled out by an American philosopher as one of Sartre's most unique contributions. "What the existentialist admires," noted Grene, "is not the happiness of a man's life, the goodness of his disposition or the rightness of his acts, but the authenticity of his existence."[66]

One reason that Sartre's conception of authenticity gained increasing respectful attention was the growing sense that the value of individualism was threatened. "Authenticity" seemed a possible antidote for what some perceived as a new American inclination to submerge the individual self in the crowd. Social critics like Riesman were predicting dire consequences resulting from the supposed demise of the inner-directed American, and some philosophers agreed. But J. Glenn Gray, a philosophy professor at Colorado College who in later years explored the interconnections between existentialism and student protest movements, argued that no matter how much Americans talked fondly about individualism in the mid–twentieth century, they really valued the social, external self more than the inner-directed person.

Gray noted that American philosophers frequently were attracted to Sartre's emphasis on individualism and authenticity and paid them verbal homage but, in actuality, Gray believed many philosophers were largely opposed to Sartre's highly interiorized versions of these values. American philosophers, in Gray's view, favored individualism, but only a highly domesticated and socialized version of it. Ultimately, Sartreanism was "too bleak, too extreme, above all, too individualistic for us." Although Gray recognized, along with many other critics, that the French philosophy neglected the social dimensions of existence, he felt that Americans were philosophically ripe for the Sartrean emphasis on inner being: "The hard tasks of self-examination and self-evaluation are certainly as vital, in this age as in any preceding, and it may be existentialism's mission to make this evident."[67] The concept of authenticity, which represented a turning away from the social self, might provide a new fountain of spiritual nourishment badly needed in an era when the social faiths of politics and religion were found wanting. Other philosophers noted that the idea of authenticity seemed especially timely in light of the alienating nature of an increasingly technological and corporate Western society.[68]

Sartrean "authenticity" not only suited some philosophers' sense of the need to find principles within their discipline to reaffirm individualism but it also fit the shift in emphasis from existence in general to a greater focus on the human level of existence. John Smith's desire for an integrative approach that merged these perspectives was not an isolated wish—it echoed in the philosophical community. In sum, Americans often agreed that Sartrean morality offered provocative ethical guidelines, but they did not overlook its weak philosophical underpinnings, including the inability to derive universal freedom from individual freedom in a logical manner, and the failure to clarify the method by which a person might make an ethical choice. These shortcomings would continue to worry American philosophers in later years.

* * *

Sartreanism brought novel ideas and approaches into the American philosophical community during the first years of contact, and in the second stage it also began to leave its mark on the structure of that community. During the late 1940s and early 1950s, courses on Sartreanism first appeared in philosophy departments, papers on Sartre were read at meetings and conventions, and existentialism became the topic of discussion in a prestigious lecture series. In a small way, Sartreanism also created some teaching and writing opportunities for philosophers just beginning their careers.

While French existentialism was undoubtedly mentioned in contemporary philosophy courses prior to 1948, a survey of courses offered through the philosophy departments of major American colleges and universities suggests that the earliest classes that made Sartrean thought a primary focus appeared that year. One such course was taught by Wahl at the University of Chicago: "Philosophies of Existence: Phenomenology and Existentialism." John Randall and Paul Tillich team-taught another class that dealt with Sartreanism, "The Human Situation," at Columbia in 1949.[69] Like Wahl, Tillich was a visiting scholar, and this course was also a special offering.

Barnes remembered the genesis of her course on existentialism at the University of Toledo in 1950, one of the first in the United States. Barnes's class was one of the earliest taught by an American-born philosopher, and it signaled the end of dependency on foreign-born scholars to teach Sartreanism. When an inquisitive student in Barnes's beginning philosophy class asked in the spring of 1949, "What is this existentialism everyone is talking about?" Barnes, as she later recalled, "gave an inadequate answer based on a bit of secondhand reading I had done and then felt rather ashamed of myself and thought I ought to read some of the primary material and make up my own mind."[70] Feeling an immediate affinity for Sartre's position, Barnes asked to teach a course on Sartreanism the following spring.

Classes on Sartre were still few and far between in the late 1940s and early 1950s, however, and they certainly did not redirect the curriculum of philosophy departments. An extreme example of the lack of impact on logicians and some analytic philosophers occurred at Harvard. Although John Wild introduced a course entitled "The Philosophy of Man" in 1951 that dealt with contemporary existentialism, and although he continued to add other courses in later years, some professors were so immersed in their specialties that they did not remember such classes. Willard Quine, the dean of twentieth-century American logic, recalled: "I have not been aware of responses to the existentialists on the part of my philosophy colleagues or students."[71] Analogously, existentialism was introduced as a topic into a prestigious lecture series in American philosophy during this period, but the subject certainly did not eclipse other topics. Sartreanism per se was never the main focus, yet in 1950 Tillich discussed existentialism in the influential Terry Lectures at Yale.[72]

Another source of information came by way of survey classes on contemporary philosophy. Here discussions of Sartre's ideas sometimes had a powerful impact. Joseph Fell, a philosophy professor at Bucknell University who later made existentialism and phenomenology his specialties, vividly remembered his introduction to Sartreanism in a survey taught by John Miller at Williams College in Massachusetts in 1951. Because of his own historical idealism, Miller found a great deal of significance in existentialism. He took the rather Hegelian view of philosophic development, arguing that particular stances followed one another by a process of revision that preserved the meritorious in earlier views as it abandoned their deficiencies. From this perspective, Miller saw existentialism as "conserving certain unimpugnable features of modern thought—Cartesianism, naturalism, idealism—but as passing onto its successors a problem characteristic of the contemporary period."[73]

Miller argued that existentialism recognized that the subject insisted on an object that reflected its own will and meaning, but stressed a confrontation in which the subject faced the object's resistance; how could philosophy simultaneously respect "the human will to meaning and nature's independence of human designs?"[74] Miller saw existentialism as an extremely significant movement in the effort to regraft human significance onto current philosophical inquiry. The importance of this contemporary interest in the conflict between human meaning and nature's resistance deeply impressed Fell as an undergraduate in 1951. Indeed, Fell adopted this interpretive framework when he made Sartreanism a primary focus in later years.

Another influential channel through which ideas circulated within the philosophical environment was professional meetings and conventions. During this second stage of contact, papers on Sartre began to surface. Barnes remembered the exciting reception given her essay "Existentialism: Positive Contributions" at a joint meeting of the Ohio and Indiana philosophical associations at Earlham College in 1951. Not everyone agreed with the proposition that existentialism made any positive contributions, Barnes noted, "but the effect was electrifying and [the paper] dominated the discussion for the rest of the session." Maxine Greene, a professor at Columbia University who made the philosophy of education her focus, recalled a sexist component of the negative response to the papers she delivered to the Philosophy of Education Society in the 1950s: "I found great hostility to Sartre and existentialist thought and also found people identifying them with the 'soft' and the 'literary' and even the 'non-cognitive' and then making a rather short leap from that judgment to my being a woman."[75]

Sartreanism's initial entry into philosophical meetings met with the same sort of checkered reception that the doctrine received when introduced into philosophy department curricula. The emotional and vociferous reaction of philosophers reflected the struggle to come to terms with the still novel and sometimes startling Sartrean perspectives. Natanson, who was one of the first leaders in Sartrean scholarship in America and therefore privy to some of the hostile early responses, never forgot the conviction with which Radoflav Tsanoff, a philosopher at Rice University, announced at a meeting of professors teaching at midwestern and southern universities, "Sartre is a lizard!"[76]

The arrival of the French philosophy also provided a limited number of teaching and writing opportunities. As with any new body of thought, its masters were initially in short supply. The philosophers who became interested in Sartre's ideas tended to be younger—women and men just beginning their careers. Indeed, something of a generational divide characterized the American response, partly because it did provide a few individuals with some professional opportunities.

Another source of the generation gap may have been a greater inclination on the part of younger philosophers to view the world less sanguinely than did their older colleagues; the younger philosophers were people who had experienced the Depression and World War II in the impressionable and idealistic years of early adulthood. And it was the younger group who tended to be introduced to Sartreanism before they had become deeply immersed and professionally associated with other philosophical schools. Their senior colleagues typically confronted Sartre's ideas as scholars with well-established opposing philosophical perspectives.

Female philosophers, in particular, found Sartreanism a tiny window of opportunity in the male world of academic philosophy at midcentury because it did provide some teaching and writing possibilities. In comparison to the job openings for those whose skills were honed in analytic philosophy, however, positions for people specializing in Continental thought were few and far between. Female philosophers wrote a disproportionate number of the scholarly articles on Sartre published in the late 1940s and early 1950s; Barnes, Coolidge, Greene, Grene, and Rau all took advantage of their knowledge of existentialism to produce sought-after Sartrean criticism.

Like some of their male peers, women philosophers at times became involved in Sartreanism not because they agreed with its philosophical stance but because it created a window that might not otherwise have existed. Grene's experience illustrated this aspect of the relationship between the entrance of a new doctrine and fledgling professional philosophers. Sent to Freiburg as a German-American Exchange Fellow in 1931, Grene studied under Heidegger and Jaspers. Although she disliked many of the ideas of German existentialism, she wrote her dissertation on it because "it was still a new topic in this country, and I wanted to get out fast and start teaching . . . in the middle of the Depression."[77] Grene hoped the novelty of her dissertation topic would increase job opportunities.

Grene's difficulty in finding a job was not unusual in 1937, but her gender compounded the problem. The attitude she encountered was "Good-bye, you're a bright little girl but nobody gives jobs to women in philosophy."[78] Grene was finally hired by the University of Chicago, only to lose the position six years later. After her dismissal, Grene began producing Sartrean criticism. When asked why she had written so much on a strain of philosophy that she basically disagreed with, Grene remembered, "It was simple really. After I lost my job, I thought I should do anything more or less respectable I was given a chance to do." And being a woman in an almost all-male discipline made her more willing to accept anything that was offered. Grene recalled: "Women of my generation, like those of the countless generations preceding us, did what we had a chance to do, not necessarily what we were inwardly committed to doing."[79]

The thorny problems of sexual discrimination in her profession were factors that affected her relation to Sartreanism in Grene's case. The American woman who in 1948 published the first major study of Sartrean ethics in English, *Dreadful Freedom,* did so because she was trying to maintain her own legitimacy within her profession and because writing was an option when job opportunities were limited. Other women also found that Sartreanism offered possibilities. Both Barnes and Rau agreed that familiarity with existentialist doctrines, coupled with their ability to translate French, opened doors for them that might otherwise have remained closed.[80]

* * *

To summarize the preceding arguments, between 1948 and 1952 Sartreanism won increasing acceptance in the American philosophical community as a significant strain of thought. This is not to say that it was universally or uncritically embraced, but there was a shift away from the dismissive view that Sartre deserved little consideration to the opinion that some of his ideas might merit further study. Another aspect of Sartreanism's development was Americans' increasing awareness of the breadth of the philosophy's concerns. Publication of such works as *The Psychology of the Imagination* demonstrated Sartre's interest in areas on the border between psychology and philosophy, as well as his involvement in aesthetic theory.

These years also saw continued strong resistance to Sartreanism because of its opposition to the empirical and analytic bent of the mainstream in American philosophy. But coincidentally, some philosophers were willing to consider a possible rapprochement in which Sartreanism's attention to the human level of existence could be preserved without completely negating empirical and analytic methods. While opposition to Sartre's antiempirical, antianalytic approach persisted, so did philosophers' initial receptivity to its emphasis on personal freedom and responsibility. And in this period, Sartrean authenticity was favorably discussed by more than one philosopher.

What accounts for the new configurations in American philosophers' response to Sartrean thought? Certainly, the simple benevolence of the passage of time had something to do with its increased legitimacy, providing as it did an opportunity for knowledge to deepen. And the increasing dominance of analytic methodology brought in its wake philosophic backlashes that indirectly supported Sartrean perspectives too.

Some American thinkers were very worried that a narrow focus on empirical and analytic methods caused philosophers to bury their heads in the sands of philosophical technique rather than to address broad questions of human relevance. In his presidential address to the Eastern Division of the American Philosophical Association in 1945, William Wright, a professor at Dartmouth whose specialties included ethics, contrasted "minute-minded" philosophers to "magnanimous-minded" thinkers and urged his colleagues to become the latter. "Minute-minded" philosophers, said Wright, "seek to know more and more about less and less," while the "magnanimous-minded" attempted to integrate scientific knowledge with the philosophical concerns of human existence.[81] Wright's fear that the intricacy of empirical and analytic perspectives would divert philosophers' attention from issues that more directly affected human experience echoed throughout the second stage of contact with Sartreanism, encouraging philosophers to look at the French philosophy more sympathetically precisely because it did not submerge individual existence. A growing concern for the human level of meaning, and an accompanying rejection of a priori ethics, gave point to Sartre's doctrines.

Global politics also affected the American reaction. These years of the Cold War's intensification brought more ambiguity to philosophers' perception of Sartre's political behavior. A small number were hearty supporters of the growth of internationalism in philosophical pursuits within the American philosophical community. For people like McKeon, a delegate and philosophical adviser to UNESCO, the rapprochement of opposing ideas was the key to international political peace. McKeon sought ways of reconciling and amalgamating Sartreanism with the scientific traditions of Anglo-American philosophy.

Other Americans were more concerned about Sartre's political fence-sitting between democratic socialism and the Stalinist-led Communist Party. Barrett and Hook revealed the shades of gray in philosophers' attitudes. While both criticized Sartre's sometime willingness to blink at Stalinist oppression, Barrett, at least, also recognized his opposing inclination to speak out against totalitarianism. Sartre's wavering reaction to the Communist Party certainly was reflected in the ambiguous American response to him. His political straddling, combined with his increasingly strident criticism of American foreign policy in Europe, produced a political fault line among philosophers. On one side were those who saw virtue in Sartre's antitotalitarianism; on the other were those who were suspicious of his ties with the Communist Party.

The outcropping of old-new complaints among social theorists began to impact American thinkers' reactions too. The growing conviction among social critics that individual freedom and responsibility were disappearing in America made Sartre's call for the rejuvenation of those virtues in France appealing. These emerging concerns about the sublimation of the individual within a faceless, soulless crowd gave significance to Sartre's concept of authenticity that would continue to deepen.

Sartrean thought gained a share of legitimacy in this second phase of contact. As the philosophy grew familiar, its variation from the principles and method of empiricism and analysis became more apparent and troublesome too. But at the same time, more philosophers were becoming aware of the centrality of human meaning and experience in their discipline, and they recognized that Sartreanism spoke directly to those concerns. The question that began to emerge was how to winnow out valuable Sartrean perspectives from what was perceived as philosophical chaff.

4

Sartrean Paradoxes, 1952–1956

In 1950 Rice, the chair of the Kenyon College philosophy department and one of the leading exponents of existentialist thought in America, posed a question that would soon become the key issue of the mid-1950s. Rice wondered whether it made more sense to treat existentialist thought as "a kind of metaphysical tone poem" or as a philosophy in the sense of "an attempt at logically-ordered discourse." Between 1952 and 1956, philosophers began to grapple more seriously with the problem of integrating existentialist insights into the more traditional concept of philosophy. And it was during these years that awareness of Sartreanism as a serious effort to formulate a solid doctrine of being finally became widespread among American philosophers. As Sartre's translator and as an existentialist, Barnes noted happily in her 1956 introduction to *Being and Nothingness:* "It is a long time since serious philosophers have had to waste time and energy in showing that his [Sartre's] philosophy is more than the unhappy reactions of France to the Occupation and post-war distress."[1]

While many philosophers in the earlier stages clearly recognized that the existentialist focus on human subjectivity and existence was a much-needed corrective, few attempts were made to analyze in fine and lengthy detail the pathways that might lead to a workable rapprochement—the development of a productive relationship between the empirical and analytical orientation of American philosophy and the existentialist and phenomenological overtones of European thought. Philosophers began to explore with greater depth and disciplinary rigor the degree to which Sartreanism validly challenged, or could be incorporated into, the logical and deductive method of philosophizing in the mid-1950s.

The effort to answer these questions brought out so many problems that the very heart of this phase became a confrontation with the contradictions and paradoxes of Sartreanism. In that focus on ambiguity and puzzlement within the human condition, American philosophers' angle of criticism was of a piece with scholarship throughout the humanities at midcentury. Sartre also emerged as a kind of touchstone by which some philosophers in the United States implicitly defined their philosophical positions, political commitments, and vision of the proper social role of the philosopher. Sartre's insistence on active political involvement and his detachment from academia were ingredients not often incorporated into Americans' perceptions of the philosopher's function.

Barnes's completion in 1956 of the massive project of translating *L'Être et le néant* brought to a close the initial context in which Sartrean thought met the American philosophical environment—an environment in which Sartrean study was drastically limited by lack of accessibility. Barnes's translation provided a new milieu that held the promise of a broader-based, more informed scholarship. The process of legitimization that continued after 1952 was also fueled by the additional translation of more of Sartre's philosophical studies; in fact, the publication of English versions of Sartre's philosophical rather than literary works was characteristic of the mid-1950s. *Being and Nothingness* stood out as the essential new text, but others played a role too. Barnes published two sections of that volume in 1953 under the title *Existential Psychoanalysis*. Walter Kaufmann's inclusion of Sartre's philosophical and literary work in *Existentialism from Dostoevsky to Sartre* (1956), a collection of excerpts from existentialist-minded writers, was particularly important because of the extensive audience Kaufmann's text achieved.[2] Kaufmann's anthology placed Sartrean philosophy in the hands of thousands of students enrolled in survey courses in contemporary philosophy. It was eagerly adopted by philosophers who needed a readable text for their students.

The Princeton professor's book was also influential because it offered an honest and thought-provoking critique. Kaufmann, a native of Freiburg who was well versed in Continental thought, provided a lucid description of the historical roots of existentialism and the contributions of its leading philosophers. But more important, he explained and tried to refute what he believed were American philosophers' principal objections to existentialism. Kaufmann attributed much of his colleagues' dissatisfaction with Sartre's ideas to the unacademic tone of existentialism. But, noted Kaufmann, an academic existentialism would be a complete contradiction in terms; one of the wellsprings of existentialism was its opposition to rarefied philosophizing. Other issues that he knew were sources of irritation were Sartre's fondness for café life and his willingness to discuss human sexuality. Sartre's atheism, pessimism, and disavowal of Anglo-American analytic philosophy were also serious complaints.[3] By suggesting the logical weaknesses and parochialism of some of the most common criticisms, Kaufmann helped bring about a more sympathetic understanding of Sartre. The demand for *Existentialism from Dostoevsky to Sartre* was so great that a second printing came on the heels of the first, and Kaufmann's informative text was in its sixteenth printing by 1960.

The number of American philosophers producing articles on Sartre increased at middecade and, to a lesser degree, so did book-length critiques. Now more philosophers representing many different perspectives offered their assessments: naturalists, realists, idealists, logicians, and analytic philosophers. The increase in translated works meant that French fluency became less of a factor in philosophical scholarship. The ability to read French well, however, would always be an asset because it gave Americans a much better feel for the flesh and blood as well as the intellectual nuances of Sartrean concepts; fluency also enabled people to keep fully abreast of critical shifts in Sartre's quick-paced ideas and activities.

* * *

The major new topic in Sartrean scholarship in the United States in the mid-1950s was existential psychoanalysis. Sartre's formulation of the psychoanalytic arm of existentialism owed much to the work of Jaspers, Heidegger, and Ludwig Binswanger. Jaspers challenged the positivistic approach of conventional psychotherapy as overly deterministic—too willing to believe that the outcome of an individual's life was inevitable. He argued that it was incorrect to assume that personality could be adequately studied through empirical scrutiny alone; such an investigation could not, for example, reveal the existence of freedom of choice.[4]

The works of Heidegger and Binswanger were significant Sartrean influences too. Binswanger, a Swiss psychiatrist, writer, and professor at Jena in East Germany, was the most important disciple of Heidegger's thought in the field of psychotherapy. His *Daseinanalyse* (existential analysis) derived its understanding of modes of consciousness from Heidegger. Binswanger criticized one of Freud's major concepts; while Freud saw the neurotic symptom as the product of a previous traumatic experience buried in the unconscious, Binswanger felt neurosis should be explained within the context of consciousness. He viewed psychic abnormalities as an effect of a patient's distorted self-image and inadequate relation to the world. Binswanger urged his clients to become fully conscious of themselves as total people uniquely existing in a concrete reality.[5]

Sartre, too, adopted the principle of analyzing behavior in terms of its conscious meaning for the individual. He employed the doctrine of intentionality to challenge causal theories of action and emotion. While he rejected the Freudian theory of the unconscious, he accepted some facets of Freudian technique, including the belief that the years of childhood were particularly critical in the formulation of personality.[6]

One of the earliest considerations of Sartre's existential psychoanalysis presented by a philosopher in America was Alfred Stern's *Sartre: His Philosophy and Existential Psychoanalysis* (1953).[7] Born in Vienna and well schooled in existentialism and phenomenology, Stern immigrated to the United States after serving in the French army in World War II. He began teaching philosophy and languages in 1945 at the California Institute of Technology. Stern's evaluation of Sartrean psychoanalysis was suggestive of ways in which some philosophers who opposed Sartre on logical grounds responded to Sartre's perspective.

Stern focused on the illogical and paradoxical side of Sartrean psychoanalysis; he stressed both the absolutist vein in Sartre's existentialism and the ambiguity of Sartrean freedom. Sartre's version of freedom, argued Stern, did not produce an escape from anxiety, and that was its crippling weakness. Instead of relieving individuals of worry, Sartre asked them to confront it by acknowledging the self as the provider of meaning.

Stern labeled Sartre's perspective a psychiatric representation of absolute ethical idealism and irrationalism. The absolute value of anxiety was affirmed for its own sake as the highest moral principle with little regard for the effect upon the individual. Existential psychoanalysis was an irrationalism in Stern's view because he considered it unlikely that people would choose to pursue the anxiety that attended the realization of freedom from given values. In short, Sartre offered a psychoanalysis with an admiral view of the individual's potential but without a sensible pathway to achieve that pinnacle of authenticity.[8]

Wilfrid Desan, a native of Belgium and then a young philosophy professor at Kenyon College, reached similar conclusions in *The Tragic Finale: An Essay on the Philosophy of Jean-Paul Sartre* (1954).[9] Desan, like Natanson, was a path breaker in providing a detailed analysis of Sartre's ontology; his study was very much in line with the dominant impulse at middecade to examine Sartrean philosophy as a systematic whole. Like Natanson's critique, *The Tragic Finale* was an important work among those interested in Continental thought because it was another early attempt to offer a comprehensive criticism. "*The Tragic Finale,*" Desan later observed, "never made the claim to be the last word on Sartre, but it was a lucid introduction to existentialism, and became in its own way a bestseller."[10]

Desan addressed Sartre's attempt to solve the problem of being on a phenomenological basis and found it wanting; in the process, he also questioned Sartrean psychoanalysis. Like Stern, Desan pointed out that this psychoanalysis was not intended to deliver individuals from psychic pain but to validate Sartre's position that human existence was a fruitless search for being. Desan found Sartre's phenomenological descriptions novel but weakened by subjectivity; there was too much Sartre, and too little of the patient, in this analysis. A case in point was Sartre's ontological description of objects and qualities. Desan dismissed as too tenuous the association between viscosity and being that Sartre drew, as well as some of the other connections Sartre made between objects and their qualities: "Why cannot my original aversion to the viscous be the result of my personal feeling for cleanliness and hygiene rather than my fear of getting engulfed? I hate the viscid, because it endangers my white hands and my clean shirt, not because I am afraid of losing myself."[11] Existential psychoanalysis remained a peripheral aspect of Sartrean thought for American philosophers during this stage; no doubt many felt that Sartre wandered too far afield from philosophy proper, and they had little desire to follow.

* * *

The threads of established themes in the Sartrean discourse such as politics, the revolt against academic philosophy, and the relationship between subject and object continued in the mid-1950s, now embellished with additional questions and suggested answers. Sartrean politics was still not a matter of major concern to many American philosophers, but more were cognizant of Sartre's political involvements than had been earlier. Rice suggested his colleagues' slowly growing awareness in his presidential address to the Western Division of the American Philosophical Association in 1953, by using Sartre as a case history to illustrate the need for philosophers both to expand their involvement in political and social issues and to beware the dangers of overactivity. Philosophers, argued Rice, had a dual commitment to pure philosophy and to more practical matters; Sartre was "a particularly striking illustration of the general point that . . . any philosopher if he pursues one commitment very far learns that he must come to terms with both."[12]

American philosophers' response to Sartre's politics underwent a change in the beginning of this period, brought on by a shift in Sartre's alignment. Sartre increased his independent support of the French Communist Party in 1952. The catalyst was the government's harsh treatment of the party in Paris when the Communists protested both the cessation of armistice talks and anticommunist remarks made by General Matthew Ridgway, Dwight Eisenhower's successor as the Supreme Allied Commander in Europe.[13]

Sartre now tried to do everything in his power to maintain the neutrality of Europe and to oppose anticommunism. Between 1952 and 1956 he protested the Rosenbergs' execution, visited Russia (1953), and made known his support of Vietnamese nationalism (1954). He firmly denounced the Soviet Union's repression of the Hungarian revolt in 1956 but was unwilling to abandon the possibility of an independent French Communist Party.[14] These procommunist rather than antitotalitarian efforts won Sartre the limelight in America during these years. In liberal magazines like the *New Republic* and the *Partisan Review*, Sartre was cast as a contradictory neutralist who, too often, fell docilely into the arms of the Communist Party.

Sartre's and Albert Camus's ideological falling-out in 1952 also left its mark on the philosophical community. During that year Camus completed *L'Homme révolté* (*The Rebel*) in which he argued that the utopian ends of a revolution could not justify the use of violent means.[15] Camus criticized Hegel for confusing reason with fate and Marx for arguing that reason guided class struggle in the process. Finally, Camus sharply reprimanded Sartre for being too willing to follow in the footsteps of Stalinist Marxism and rejected Sartre's position that a writer should never subsume politics to literature. A negative review of *L'Homme révolté* was published in *Les Temps Modernes*, and Camus responded with anger. He belittled Sartreanism as bourgeois Marxism in a letter to Sartre, and Sartre replied by criticizing Camus for trying to destroy the Communist Party before establishing a better socialist replacement.[16]

Nicola Chiarmonte, the European editor of the *Partisan Review*, sketched a damning portrait of Sartre in his analysis of the famous debate in the magazine that gained currency. Chiarmonte angrily scolded Sartre for believing in the Marxist principle of the historical justification of revolutionary violence. Some American philosophers accepted this picture of Sartre as a Communist Party lapdog—and a schizophrenic one at that. Brand Blanshard, the dean of midcentury American rationalism at Yale University, remembered some of his colleagues' displeasure with Sartre's partial embrace of the party. Natanson later recalled, "certainly he was under suspicion for his Marxist or Communist views—even if the French Communist Party attacked him." Support of the Communist Party was a major complaint in Kaufmann's list of American philosophers' chief objections against Sartre. Kaufmann concluded that "in the United States, this is held against him more than anything else." Kaufmann, who was appreciative of many of Sartre's doctrines and who had done much to introduce Sartre to a wider audience, included himself among those who took a negative view of Sartre's politics. The Princeton professor remarked wryly: "Philosophical profundity and political sense do not always go together; on the contrary."[17]

Hook, however, believed that many of his liberal-minded colleagues in philosophy were not critical enough of Sartre's willingness to work amicably with the Communist Party. Seared by heavy-handed interrogations of his democratic socialism by Communist Party leaders in the 1930s and further repulsed by Stalin's anti-Semitism and postwar purgings, Hook stood on the outer edges of liberalism as an unrelenting critic of the reality of the Communist Party's suppression of human rights. Hook lambasted liberals in a 1952 symposium on American culture in the *Partisan Review* for their neutralism and for turning a blind eye to the flaws of European socialism and communism while endlessly criticizing American democracy. Hook characteristically minced no words: "The lowest form of intelligent life is led by left-bank American expatriates who curry favor with Sartrean neutralists by giving the lowdown on the cultural 'reign of terror' in America."[18]

Herbert Spiegelberg was one of those philosophers who Hook believed was too uncritical of Sartre's conciliatory posture toward the Communist Party. Spiegelberg spoke out against what he believed was the tendency of liberal colleagues to force Sartre into the arms of the Communists. Spiegelberg, born in Strasbourg in 1904 and trained in philosophy in Germany, was then the chair of the philosophy department at Lawrence College in Appleton, Wisconsin, and a nationally known expert on phenomenology. In "French Existentialism: Its Social Philosophies," an essay published in the *Kenyon Review* in 1954, Spiegelberg noted that "our misunderstandings, our misinterpretations, and our misrepresentations are contributing factors in driving these non-Communist groups into the Communist camp."[19] Spiegelberg's point received a limited hearing among philosophers, however, because the *Kenyon Review* was a journal targeted toward a more literary audience.

Spiegelberg came away from a visit to Paris in 1953 with the understanding that although Sartre's anti-anticommunism and critique of American foreign and domestic policy had intensified, Sartre was still committed to maintaining his distance from the Communist Party. Spiegelberg argued in the *Kenyon Review* that American philosophers ignored the adjustment in Sartre's social and political philosophy that had been under way since his involvement in Resistance activities. The chief characteristic of this change was a heightened emphasis on the existence of others as essential to the self; individual freedom was therefore dependent on the liberty of others too. Spiegelberg was quick to acknowledge that Sartre's newer position lacked the theoretical foundation of his former stance; what Spiegelberg wished to stress was not the philosophical validity of the more recent position but its very existence and the possibility of a sympathetic discussion of it by Anglo-American philosophers.

Above all, Spiegelberg wanted to counter the view of philosophers such as Hook by etching Sartre's disagreement with the Communist Party into Americans' minds and by reiterating ways in which Sartre's political values were ones with which they could agree. Spiegelberg closed his essay with the reminder: "We should never forget that existentialism also stands for belief in the unescapable, if not total, freedom and responsibility of the individual for himself as for others."[20] The Sartrean values that Spiegelberg believed American philosophers could identify with extended beyond personal liberty; they included a humanism that challenged the individual to face existence without illusion and a rejection of the orthodoxy of dialectical materialism and Stalinist totalitarianism.

The ambiguity of Sartre's political stance was sharply highlighted in the reflections of American philosophers like Spiegelberg and Hook. Spiegelberg, in emphasizing Sartre's independent critical posture, downplayed Sartre's willingness to compromise with the Communist Party and his determination to meld existentialism and Marxism. Hook recognized the reality of Sartre's currying favor with Communist Party members who were sometimes willing to tread on human rights, but he focused too narrowly on this. Still, American philosophers' conflicting assessments of Sartre's politics were understandable; his actions were ambiguous and always changing as he tried to keep his footing on the difficult path of neutralism. As a man without a party, Sartre found his political course difficult to navigate.

Another source of philosophers' dissatisfaction was simply the depth of Sartre's political involvement. Rice expressed that concern in his presidential address to the Western Division of the American Philosophical Association in 1952: "He [Sartre] is often engaged when he should be disengaged, and vice versa."[21] Here was uneasiness over Sartre's eagerness to escape the contemporary model of the philosopher as a detached scholar able to view the issues of the day dispassionately.

That uncomfortableness echoed in other criticisms stemming from Sartre's effort to disassociate himself from academic philosophy. Although Sartreanism received serious and steadily increasing consideration during these years, the argument that it was of questionable merit because it was not an academic philosophy was never entirely put to rest. Some critics expressed disgruntlement over Sartre's willingness to discard the image of philosophers as professionals who acquired philosophical legitimacy largely through their attachment to an academic institution. Natanson satirically exaggerated this view for rhetorical effect: "Who is this enfant terrible who is at once philosopher, psychologist, novelist, dramatist, commentator, editor, lecturer and disturber of the peace?" And no doubt for some, because of Sartre's mounting fame, a tinge of envy was present, as it had been in earlier stages. Morton White hinted at colleagues' jealousy in *The Age of Analysis* (1955), a popular account of the analytic bent of contemporary Anglo-American philosophy: "Sartre achieved popular fame that far exceeds anything possible for an English-speaking philosopher today." Jealousy may have bubbled up, too, in Stern's suggestion that the existentialists surrendered their philosophy of existence to wealth: "Their sacrifice has not been in vain, since it has brought them fame, and in the case of Sartre, even wealth. And this makes existence much more bearable, even for Existentialists."[22]

Sartre's readiness to include sexuality as an appropriate topic for philosophy was another facet of the charge that Sartre was unacademic. Kaufmann believed that Sartre's frank discussions of the philosophical implications of sex in *Being and Nothingness* sent more than one American philosopher into mild shock and were an important undercurrent in their cool reception. This aspect surfaced more clearly now, brought on in 1953 by the publication of *Existential Psychoanalysis,* which included chapters from *Being and Nothingness* that discussed the philosophical significance of sexual behavior. Kaufmann felt it necessary to remind readers in 1956 that Sartre's treatment of sex "is designed to increase our understanding of important problems, never to arouse desire."[23]

The comments of Stern and Albert Levi, a philosopher at Washington University who wrote extensively on the social construction of philosophy, suggested the uncomfortable reactions of some. Stern warned that parts of *Being and Nothingness* contained "pornographic passages," and Levi, whose sympathies were with Alfred North Whitehead but who was still willing to acknowledge that he had learned a great deal from Sartre, protested Sartre's "preoccupation . . . with the experience of the viscous secretions."[24] Neither Stern nor Levi ignored or dismissed out of hand Sartre's ontological analysis of sexuality in which sexual desire was the for-itself's wish to capture the other's subjectivity. They credited that theory as philosophically insightful but could not overcome the feeling that Sartre's most graphic explanations overstepped their boundaries of good taste.

* * *

More traditional themes continued to add new layers of argument and significance during this phase: the relationship between subjectivity and objectivity, freedom, the nature of being, and rapprochement with other philosophical currents. Sartre's analysis of subjectivity and objectivity previously caught the attention of Miller at Williams College and others because it confronted the contemporary problematic of a subject that insisted on an object that reflected its own meanings.[25] Philosophers like Charles Hendel, chair of the Yale philosophy department and a metaphysician, and Wild, a Harvard realist with a growing interest in phenomenology and existentialism, deepened this discussion in the mid-1950s.

Hendel advocated a new metaphysics that integrated the physical, objective mode of being with the subjective mode. In "The Subjective as a Problem," an essay that appeared in the widely read *Philosophical Review* in 1953, Hendel presented existentialism as a reassertion of human consciousness in the face of contemporary philosophy's dismissal of it. Hendel attributed consciousness' loss of primacy to the discovery of purposive behavior in nature; he believed that the popularity of naturalism as a dominant perspective in contemporary American philosophy substantially eroded the significance of human awareness in philosophy's field of vision.[26]

Wild, taking a different tack, chided analytic philosophy for being the culprit in the rise to power of a "subjectivist" tendency in American philosophy—an inclination to turn away from real objects present in experience to refocus on the conceptual and logical apparatus through which objects were perceived. Wild's *The Challenge of Existentialism* (1953) was the first book-length attempt by an American philosopher to integrate existentialism and realism.[27]

While Hendel emphasized the loss of human consciousness, Wild stressed the fading away of the object. But for both a naturalistically minded metaphysician like Hendel and a realist like Wild, existentialism brought something of value to an incomplete philosophical discourse. For Hendel saw that existentialism presented the possibility of reintroducing the importance, but not the exclusivity, of the subjective perspective. Wild hoped that the phenomenological ontology of existentialists like Sartre would return attention to objects considered in relation to their being in the world. The outcome of discussion on subject-object dualism in Sartreanism at middecade was typically a greater appreciation of Sartre's attempt to avoid the dichotomy but the conclusion was that this attempt was not entirely successful.

Of course neither Hendel nor Wild was a pioneer in recognizing that strains of existentialism held out the promise of filling in gaps in contemporary philosophy. What was new was the earnestness of their interest in combining the perspectives of Continental thought with those of Anglo-American philosophy. The conspicuously positive tone was very noticeable in both these efforts at reconciliation. Hendel stated with equanimity that existentialism was a "creative art" and "active communication." John Wild described existentialism in glowing terms. The Harvard professor concluded a bit rhapsodically that a blending of realism and existentialism saved him from the jaws of an analytic philosophy too blindly focused on the conceptual and logical structures that framed philosophical discourse: "If others like myself may be helped . . . from the provincialism of Anglo-American analysis, it will have accomplished its purpose."[28]

Hendel sounded very much like Ames, who had railed against existentialist subjectivity in the pages of the *Journal of Philosophy* two years earlier, when he argued that the existentialists "must integrate the science of the objective world with their knowledge of man" to avoid becoming part of a "psycho-therapeutic process directed by esoteric practitioners."[29] But important refinements emerged when the discussion was in Hendel's hands. While Ames outlined the difference between the empirical and existentialist perspectives with no glimmer of rapprochement in sight, Hendel took up the conversation precisely because he felt it was shocking that adherents to these two views so rarely communicated.

The Yale professor explored the relationship between existentialist thought and empirically based philosophy by pointing out that existentialists did not so much discard scientific knowledge as show little interest in it. He observed that existentialists often agreed that science had truth-value for the individual immersed in daily existence and so were in line with the pragmatic tradition; existentialists were content with the existence of two very different types of truth, while many American philosophers were not.[30]

Hendel was not even unsettled by Sartre's declaration that the universe was absurd. He explained that Sartre did not mean to deny the rationality of the world as it was expressed in scientific principles, but to remind us, as Hume did, that the universe was not an unchanging system with fixed laws. While Hendel clarified the distinctions that the existentialists made among different kinds of truth, his final reservation was still that of many another American philosopher—the existentialists needed to incorporate knowledge of the objective world into their understanding of the individual.[31] Wild added that the existentialists and phenomenologists made significant achievements in establishing the intentional nature of experience, modes of temporality, and the separation of the human being from the categories of idea or scientific organism.[32] The task that lay ahead, Wild argued in *The Challenge of Existentialism,* was to fill in the holes with the methodology of realism; the phenomenological method was incomplete and there was no philosophy of nature.

Here again in Hendel and Wild were all the usual complaints about existentialism, so often repeated that they seemed almost obligatory. The negative critique was essentially the same; the difference was the level of interest in the possibility of integrating Anglo-American philosophy and Continental thought. These philosophers were probing deeply into the principles of existentialism, and by doing that they found congruities with other points of view and removed some unnecessary obstructions. Hendel broke down the common assumption that existentialism precluded the acceptance of the instrumental value of science. Wild was the first American to devote an entire book to an explanation of how an empirically minded perspective like realism could coexist with existentialism. And both philosophers were interested in expanding the list of fruitful existentialist inquiries.

Interest in exploring the links between existentialism and analytic philosophy cropped up among other philosophers too. White suggested the possibility of reconciliation in *The Age of Analysis.* And George Schrader presented commonalities of existentialism and analytic thought in "Existence, Truth and Subjectivity," an essay included in the *Journal of Philosophy*'s publication of papers read at "Existential Thought and Contemporary Philosophy in the West," a symposium held at the 1956 meeting of the Eastern Division of the American Philosophical Association.[33] Schrader, a Yale metaphysician whose interests included ethics and existentialism, continued to pay attention to the relationship between metaphysics, philosophical analysis, and Continental thought throughout his career.

White and Schrader agreed that the most obvious point of contact between analytic philosophy and existentialism was an interest in human existence. The emphasis linguistic philosophers placed on analyzing the language of the ordinary individual implied that concern. White observed that "even the language of the existentialists, which seems so difficult to our ears, has its English translators, and, I think its affinities with developments in England and America." Schrader added that philosophical analysis "seems to be based upon an implicit appeal to the wisdom, and virtue of the common man."[34] Noting that as yet the method of analytic philosophy had no doctrines that limited it to one subject, he proposed that it could choose to tackle human existence too.

Finally, all these efforts at rapprochement were significant because of the particular philosophical environments from which they came. Hendel and Schrader were professors at Yale, and White and Wild taught at Harvard. That a genuinely appreciative, though by all means critical, attitude toward Sartre could emerge from Yale was not too surprising because of that department's history of metaphysical inquiry, but the metaphysical side of Sartreanism—phenomenological ontology—was, after all, an attempt to overturn the traditional metaphysical methodology that incorporated logic and deduction. Sartre carefully distinguished between metaphysics as the study of the origins of being and ontology as the study of the description of the structures of being. He did not disapprove of metaphysical inquiry but, by his own definition, he did not engage in it.[35]

More surprising was the emergence of Wild's and White's tolerant books and articles from Harvard, where some members of the department were very well known for their fervent embrace of logic and analytic thought. Wild's and White's interest in existentialism and phenomenology testified most directly to the dedication of individuals within the American philosophical community to the principle of free inquiry and diversity of opinion, for the environment at Harvard was not very nurturing to currents beyond the mainstream of Anglo-American thought.

Sartreanism was certainly not wholeheartedly embraced at Harvard or, for that matter, at any of the other major training grounds for American philosophers such as Columbia, Yale, Princeton, or the University of Chicago, but these settings also did not completely stifle Sartrean scholarship. To some degree, the materialization of interested philosophers at these institutions constituted another small rite of passage in the evolution of Sartreanism; even in America's most prestigious philosophy departments where strong traditions of analysis, empiricism, and naturalism held sway, a few voices expressed an honest interest in Continental thought. An even stronger involvement in existentialism and phenomenology was under way in a few schools of lesser size and status, and by the mid-1950s a small network of philosophy departments sympathetic to Continental influences flourished. At places like Kenyon College, Northwestern University, and the New School for Social Research, philosophers and their students knew they could find a supportive environment for the contemplation of existentialism.

* * *

Particular topics in the Sartrean framework also found a wider audience in the mid-1950s. Freedom was always a favorite subject in the American discourse, but now it was pondered in great detail. The centrality of freedom to Sartreanism was clear: Human being, as consciousness, was in a dialectical relationship with nonhuman being. The for-itself, or consciousness, was freedom from the massive fullness of being-in-itself; it was lack and desire—nothingness. Although it hungered for the fullness of being, it never attained its goal. The acts and choices of the for-itself were free, and the individual was forced into self-definition because of the absence of absolutes; conscious acceptance of this freedom established authentic existence.[36] The Sartrean dialectic between the free self and the historical situation in *Being and Nothingness* was essentially paradoxical.[37] Sartre stressed in *Existentialism* that the subject was "in situation," and this implied the possibility of limiting freedom. But it was the self that gave meaning to the situation by choosing its significance; in that sense, it retained individual freedom even in the midst of restrictions. To the extent that decisions affected other people, individuals chose for other people too.[38]

The philosophical discourse on Sartrean freedom moved to a new level in the mid-1950s. More philosophers took up Sartre's argument on its own terms and dealt with the problems involved in the limited type of liberty Sartre considered—that modicum of internal freedom that endured, regardless of existential constraints. Now the dominant vision of freedom in American philosophy more frequently confronted an accurate definition of Sartrean freedom, and Americans began to see some virtues in Sartre's view because the two models were no longer diametrically opposed by Sartre's supposed disregard for environmental constraints. William Earle of Northwestern University clarified the point in "Freedom and Existence," an essay written in 1955 for a symposium on freedom and existence in the *Review of Metaphysics:* "We are not then talking about freedom as it can be thought of in the physical world. . . . We are trying to characterize that internal freedom which is the source of our acts and is never found in the physical world."[39] Earle was then beginning his career at Northwestern, where interest in existentialism and phenomenology ran high. He received his Ph.D. from the University of Chicago in 1951 and included among his specialties Hegelianism, existentialism, and aesthetics. Earle would become well known for his investigations into the relationship between existentialism and religion in later years.

But even when Sartrean freedom was examined within its own parameters as personal freedom, which more American philosophers were now inclined to do, philosophers found problems. In *The Tragic Finale,* Desan criticized Sartre's position that the for-itself's radical freedom was based on a complete rejection of the ego. The tremendous activity of the for-itself, Desan contended, and the existence of a sense of personal identity, implied the presence of ego; Desan rejected the concept of the for-itself's emptiness and negativity that was essential to Sartre's system.[40] Another sticking point for American philosophers was the interrelationship between Sartrean freedom and the doctrine that existence preceded essence. While maintaining that a human being was free because an inescapable part of the "human condition" was freedom, Sartre tried to hold onto the principle that this type of freedom was not an essence or absolute. Many philosophers found this distinction highly artificial.[41]

Earle was one of the few American philosophers fully comfortable with the ambiguities and paradoxes present in Sartre's concept of freedom. Earle eagerly explored the implications of a reflexive for-itself. Sartre described the for-itself as a subject that knew itself as a subject; self-consciousness did not imply a subject-object relationship. The self that was free to choose was marked by this reflexive state.[42]

Like Sartre, Earle felt an inner certainty of freedom. When he asked the origin of this belief, he called into question theories about nature rather than his perception of freedom. "Freedom is self-evident," Earle stated boldly, "the ultimate principles of nature are not." Earle argued that the sense of personal choice Sartre described simply could not be "analyzed literally without running into flat absurdities and paradoxes." The individual's idea of intelligibility was modeled on the basis of experience with the physical and prereflexive world, and thus the reflexive state of inner freedom could not be fathomed with prereflexive thinking. Earle held his ground firmly: "Such paradoxes do not mean that we don't know what we are talking about."[43] Earle found profundity in Sartre's complex view of freedom, for it offered him an impression of what an absolute might be like.

These mid-1950s affirmations and refutations of Sartrean freedom more often discriminated between the common connotation of freedom in the world and the French philosopher's description of that germ of inexpungible human choice that determined the significance that would be given to possible constraints. Criticisms were less frequently broadsides based on the existence of external forces constricting freedom. While many American philosophers uncovered the contradictions and confusions in Sartre's discussion of inner freedom, some discovered in the process that although Sartrean freedom could be maddeningly paradoxical, that very quality might provide valuable insights. They sensed that Sartre moved closer to bringing into full view the complexity of human existence because he did present an ambiguous structure of freedom. Desan, who disclosed Sartre's logical errors unsparingly, nevertheless concluded: "The technician and the pragmatist glue us to the visible world. The Existentialist, on the contrary, takes to himself all those things which others want to frustrate in us: experience of existence, experience of freedom and of its absurdity."[44]

Sartre's version of freedom also gained greater attention because it construed freedom as a liberty that could survive in a world in which threats to freedom were more apparent. The older tradition of American freedom was one in which individual liberty always seemed to be pitted against social, political, and economic forces that tried to destroy it, but Sartre presented a freedom that endured in the heart of hostile forces. Sartre's configuration was, in a sense, more sophisticated. He adapted his freedom to suit the growing recognition that social progress might not be inevitable and that evil forces that threatened liberty did exist in the world. His view of freedom was also more sophisticated because of its combined ingredients of absolutism and relativism. Sartre's radical freedom was absolute in the sense that the individual never lost the ability to say "No!" but it recognized that choices were made in a world of moral relativism. Once again the paradox of the coexistence of the qualities of absolutism and relativism added a compelling layer of complexity.

* * *

Questions about radical freedom naturally went hand in hand with Sartre's formulation of being and nonbeing, for the ontological characterization of human freedom was nonbeing. Considerations of the adequacy of Sartre's description of the dialectic between those two polarities continued to be part of the ongoing broad debate over the nature and value of metaphysical speculation. In 1953, Hook at New York University and John Randall at Columbia locked horns over being in the *Journal of Philosophy*. Although neither mentioned Sartre, the argument obliquely shed light on elements in naturalistic thought that made some philosophers open to investigations of being that might kindle interest in existentialism.

Hook's "Quest for Being" (1953) was a belated reply to Randall's *Journal of Philosophy* article, "Metaphysics: Its Function, Consequences, and Criteria" (1946).[45] What most concerned Hook was philosophers' formulations of an approach to metaphysics that did not adhere to the scientific method of observation and logical analysis. Hook was also highly skeptical of what he believed was a misguided eagerness to accept vast generalizations about something called "being."[46]

In "On Being Rejected," John Randall responded much more quickly to Hook's attack on his discussion of an adequate methodology. "Though he rejects it," said Randall bluntly, "Mr. Hook is distinctly worried by being."[47] Hook, Randall believed, too rapidly dismissed the possibility that the scientific method could be incorporated into an investigation of being. The naturalistically minded Randall credited his willingness to pursue this approach to the existential investigations of Tillich and Heidegger.

Hook, in contrast to Randall, disapproved of the generation of new philosophical language that was characteristic of the speculative thought under consideration. Like Hendel, Randall insisted that innovative expressions were particularly important in metaphysics because they helped to free philosophers from a world frozen by conventional terminology.[48] Randall was also forceful in his defense of the need to pursue overarching concepts to explain existence; he chided "the nominalistic Mr. Hook" for his reluctance to search out such ideas. Randall, however, was solidly united with Hook on one point—the danger of inquiries that strayed too far from the path of scientific method and turned "being" into a catchall answer. Here Randall clearly warned against the overly ambiguous connotation of "being" that he believed some philosophers, including Sartre, nurtured.

Randall's comments were telling because his openness to the potentially murky inquiry into being established points at which a naturalistically minded philosopher might share some perspectives with a speculative thinker such as Sartre. Sartrean elements in Randall's thought included a positive attitude toward metaphysics, a willingness to invent new philosophical language, and an openness to the construction of generalized concepts in the pursuit of broad metaphysical explanations.

Throughout the discussion of being, unsettling paradoxes in Sartreanism rose to the surface, just as they did in the discourse on politics, subjectivity, and freedom. Ultimately, they all referred back to the central question Rice had raised in 1950: Was existentialism a metaphysical tone poem or a logically ordered philosophical discourse? Much of American philosophers' concern during this stage was to answer that question, and one way of doing so was to locate Sartre's proper place within the philosophical tradition.

Although Hegel's influence on Sartrean thought had received attention earlier, in this period Sartre's indebtedness to Hegel came into much sharper focus. Greater interest in the nonidealistic aspects of Hegelianism and its dialectical configurations had already attracted many Continental philosophers, and now more Americans followed suit. Increased respect for Hegel encouraged respect for Sartre, and the emphasis on Sartre's roots in neo-Hegelianism clarified his place within the philosophical cavalcade.

But here again ambiguity flourished. Hendel observed in "The Subjective as a Problem" that "they [the existentialists] all seem to be post-Hegelians, yet resentful of their descendance."[49] Sartreanism appeared suspended between the idealistic and rationalistic qualities of Hegelianism and the existential and irrational qualities of existentialism. Full recognition of the depth of Sartre's debt to Hegel resulted in philosophers' observations that Sartreanism could flourish only where Hegelianism earned a good measure of respect and in the conclusion that Sartreanism would not spread among American philosophers until more of them engaged in a reexamination of the nonidealistic strands of the German philosophy.

And of course when Americans tried to fit Sartreanism into the logico-deductive philosophical tradition as a whole, they confronted the same paradox. It was not possible to dismiss it summarily as an expression of the disintegration of the concept of philosophy as a process involving logic, observation, and theory building with the intention of discovering universal principles; Sartre used logic when it suited his purposes, he was an advocate of the phenomenological method of observation, and his own logical inquiry clearly was evidence of rational theory formation.

Smith, who began teaching at Yale in the early 1950s, followed up his earlier essay with another one that tried to bring existentialism's relationship to the philosophical tradition into clearer view. Smith noted Sartre's rationalistic systematization in "The Revolt of Existence," an essay published in the *Yale Review* in 1954, and asked whether a systematic philosophy of existence could still be true to the original purpose of existentialism, which was to revolt against such a style.[50] He concluded that existentialism could not remain committed to its founding principles if it persisted in systematization, but if existentialism refused systematization it would be forever beyond the pale of traditional philosophy. The Yale professor believed an existentialist current like Sartreanism was at bottom an effort at ontological system building that was neither fish nor fowl; it contradicted the spirit of existentialism with its rational constructions, while its narrow focus on human existence barred its entry into the tradition of logical, deductive systematic philosophy.[51]

Although American philosophers were right in noting that Sartreanism would not easily find root in a milieu that was closely tied to logic, philosophical analysis, and empiricism, some missed the appeal of its paradoxical nature. For the ambiguity in Sartreanism had as its source the enduring paradox of human being—individuals' simultaneous residence in existence, ideas, and reason. It was the reflection of this tension in Sartreanism that helped generate the philosophy's dynamism.

* * *

Hazel Barnes finished her translation of *Being and Nothingness* in 1956, bringing to a close a period in which Sartre's complete philosophical framework was not available in English. The intellectual journey that led to Barnes's massive project revealed philosophical and ethical sympathies that encouraged some American philosophers to explore Sartre. Barnes's interest in French existentialism was sparked by a student's casual question after class one day at the University of Toledo in 1949. The commitment to Sartreanism that developed, however, was rooted in earlier turns in her intellectual history.

Born in 1915 in Wilkes-Barre, Pennsylvania, Barnes received her Ph.D. in classics from Yale. During college she revolted against the fundamentalist Free Methodism of her youth, but the rejection of that religious framework left her with a need to find an alternative philosophical viewpoint, one that would exclude Christianity but retain the principles of personal integrity and responsibility with which she had been raised.[52] Barnes's allegiance to those values of childhood made Sartre's ideas compelling. When she discussed Sartre's depiction of Orestes in *The Flies* in her introduction to *Being and Nothingness,* Barnes celebrated the young Greek prince as an existentialist hero who accepted "the tension of absolute freedom and total responsibility."[53]

Sartreanism came in the wake of Barnes's need to fill a void left by her dissatisfaction with Christianity. Her encounter with William James's *The Varieties of Religious Experience* (1936) was a significant step along the way.[54] James's study made Barnes realize that the explanation of a religious experience was rooted in the individual's unique understanding of the event and was not handed down from any other source. Barnes labeled this a "humanistic" approach, and she committed herself to it from that point on.[55] Once again, James's perspective on philosophical beliefs served to form a bridge to Sartreanism. Barnes believed that an essential and obvious precursor to a sympathetic view of Sartre was the rejection of any approach that posited absolute values; in the introduction to *Being and Nothingness* she noted that Sartre's atheism was a major source of the hostility that his philosophy encountered.[56]

The translation of *Being and Nothingness* represented the culmination of one of the underlying forces in American philosophers' responses to Sartreanism in the mid-1950s—the desire to grasp the entirety of Sartre's philosophical structure. Barnes's undertaking of this huge project was certainly fueled by that mission; Sartre, she noted approvingly, "is one of the very few twentieth-century philosophers to present us with a total system." She wanted to enable the Anglo-American philosophical community to criticize Sartre's ideas in terms of his overall structure rather than to isolate specific doctrines and debate them in a vacuum. She also hoped to temper the common objection that Sartre was a derivative thinker by pointing out his original contributions without dismissing Sartre's tendency not to footnote his indebtedness to others.[57]

The two philosophers who reviewed *Being and Nothingness* expressed appreciation for the importance of Barnes's mission. Wild of Harvard University and Barrett of New York University, both well-known advocates of Continental thought, pointed out that the publication of *Being and Nothingness* proved to their colleagues that Sartre offered a systematic philosophy. Barrett reflected that "now that we have his big book, the bible of French Existentialism, available to American readers, the most powerful impression it leaves is how much of a piece all his writing is." Wild and Barrett believed that the translation of *Being and Nothingness* established Sartre's claim to the first rank of contemporary philosophers beyond a shadow of a doubt. *Being and Nothingness* confirmed Sartreanism as a philosophy that would have to be reckoned with by the Anglo-American philosophical community, Barrett maintained, and Wild added optimistically, "Let us hope it may portend a real revival of philosophy in the western world."[58]

These statements of the strengths of Sartreanism were accompanied by clear-sighted criticisms of the philosophy's weaknesses. Wild noted bluntly that "many of Sartre's ideas are open to question," and he pinpointed radical freedom and moral relativity as concepts that would not settle easily with American philosophers.[59] But Wild himself found that Sartre's emphasis on liberty made Sartre's morality less relative, and he believed Sartre's description of consciousness as a freedom rather than a fixed entity was an important redeeming quality. Barrett concluded that the view of the human condition as a state of being condemned to freedom was "over-ingenious, one-sided, [and] dialectically clever at the expense of fact" but nevertheless saved by a beam of truth.[60]

The two reviews were striking in their similarity. The commentators agreed that the translation of *Being and Nothingness* established Sartreanism as a systematic perspective that philosophers could not summarily dismiss, but it was one whose principal concepts were fraught with philosophical problems. Their conclusions reflected both the new recognition that Sartreanism was a cohesive formulation and the endurance of the judgment pronounced when Sartreanism was first introduced in America—that the key doctrines upon which the framework depended were highly problematic. Wild and Barrett, although existentialist sympathizers, produced the answer that many other philosophers gave to Rice's query: Sartreanism was an attempt at systematic philosophy, but much of its real value lay in its quality as a metaphysical tone poem that evoked the anxious state of the mid–twentieth-century self seeking value, freedom, and responsibility.

* * *

Sartrean scholarship in the American philosophical community matured considerably between 1952 and 1956. The number of books and articles written by philosophers grew, and in 1955 *The Review of Metaphysics* offered a symposium on freedom and existentialism. The next year the *Journal of Philosophy* published the American Philosophical Association's symposium on existentialism and contemporary Anglo-American thought. Prominent philosophers like Hendel, Schrader, Smith, and White found existentialism important enough to merit their attention, and they discerned positive attributes in it.

One result of the expanded commentary was increased recognition that the French philosophy sought a solid doctrine of being on which to anchor an image of the individual. This was precisely the point that Natanson had argued forcefully for in 1951, but it was not fully assimilated until the mid-1950s. The expansion of scholarship also brought in its wake increased awareness of Sartreanism's roots in such diverse strains of thought as Hegelianism and phenomenology—in short, a more general appreciation of Sartreanism's deep ties to other traditions in the history of philosophy. But greater consciousness of well-established connections did not make it easier to slip Sartreanism smoothly into the philosophical cavalcade because the traditions on which Sartreanism relied were sometimes oppositional. When philosophers confronted the question of whether Sartreanism should be evaluated as logically ordered discourse or as a tone poem, the unavoidably ambiguous answer was "a little bit of both."

Sartrean paradoxes also came to the foreground as American philosophers delved deeper into specific problems and doctrines. They confronted equivocal construction, for example, in Sartre's concept of "the human condition." On the one hand, the term implied that individuals possessed universal characteristics of freedom and responsibility, but on the other hand, no absolute human nature was established.

Reflections on Sartreanism's proper place within the philosophical tradition and the uncovering of misleading rhetoric and ambiguity in some of Sartre's central doctrines led American thinkers to the contradictory core at the heart of the French philosophy. The majority were not at all pleased to find confusion on the philosophical plane, but on a social and cultural level, Sartreanism's ideas had undeniable resonance. Sartre's description of the individual as hopeful of reaching the perfection of a God yet eager to live in the untroubled, insentient manner of a stone, as a projection toward freedom while a captivator of others' freedom, was in synchrony with the sense of cultural paradox stemming from the simultaneous progression of science and technology, the persistence of the human aptitude for evil, and uncertainty about the existence of absolute moral values. Melvin Rader, a philosopher at the University of Washington whose interests included the intersection of literature, ethics, and philosophy, focused on this sense of crisis in his opening address to the convention of the Pacific Division of the American Philosophical Association in 1952: "We have fathomed many of the secrets of the universe; we have invented the mechanical means to wipe out poverty and to build a world community; but we have attained no corresponding cultivation of feeling and no adequate spiritual assimilation."[61]

Desire for the infusion of specific existentialist tenets into other philosophical viewpoints was spreading in the mid-1950s. Analytic philosophers like White, realists like Wild, and naturalists like Randall all believed in the soundness of merging some of the concepts and methodologies of existentialism with the dominant currents of empiricism and analysis in Anglo-American philosophy. The impetus for this union came chiefly from the widely held opinion that contemporary Anglo-American discourse was incomplete and that it needed the enrichment that existentialism offered. In *The Age of Analysis*, White noted the paramount importance of communication and cross-fertilization between Anglo-American and Continental thought: "So long as we think of philosophy as a tightly compartmentalized subject in which there are Sartres who move us and Carnaps who prove for us, we are bound to see the philosophical world torn by something far more depressing than disagreement." For White, that destructive element was the inability and reluctance of philosophers of both traditions to exchange ideas with one another. Randall made the focus of his 1956 presidential address to the Eastern Division of the American Philosophical Association the need to expand the restricted vision of analytic philosophy to include an awareness of the world and the human problems in it. To emphasize his point, Randall offered a wry evaluation of analytic philosophers: "They do it so well that the only question one is left with is why on earth are they doing it at all?"[62]

Although analytic philosophy was the fad of the 1950s, some of the most esteemed voices in American philosophy objected to its tendency to speak a language known only to its devotees and to eschew philosophical problems that were also tied to the realm of social and political activity. Ernest Nagel, one of the most influential naturalistically minded philosophers of the era, expressed the power of the idea that the existentialists' concern for human problems should be blended with other perspectives in a roundabout way. By the mid-1950s Nagel found the challenge of existentialism and speculative philosophy in general so strong that he felt he had to defend naturalism. Nagel complained in his 1954 presidential address to the Eastern Division of the American Philosophical Association that some existentialists and speculative philosophers wrongly charged naturalism with insensitivity toward human values and a shallow optimism regarding the potential of science as an instrument of social progress. He observed in naturalism's defense that while it maintained that knowledge was secured through the application of a logical method, the perspective included the recognition that the world could also be encountered in other ways. "It is a matter of record," Nagel claimed passionately, "that outstanding exponents of naturalism . . . have exhibited an unequaled and tender sensitivity to the aesthetic and moral dimensions of human experience."[63] Here Nagel presented philosophers of naturalism as moral paragons.

Another source for encouraging Continental and Anglo-American discourse came from the social and political plane. Some American philosophers remained firmly committed to internationalism in philosophy, both as a way of fertilizing philosophy cross-culturally and as a means of salving political wounds by fostering global philosophical communication. The American Philosophical Association's Committee on International Cooperation during this period actively supported the Division of Philosophy and the Humanities within UNESCO and encouraged international journals and congresses.

Rice's suggestion of the possibility of an "American existentialism" during his presidential address to the Western Division of the American Philosophical Association in 1954 symbolized a high point in this blossoming interest in promoting more dialogue between advocates of analytic philosophy and Continental thought during the mid-1950s. This was the first time that the two words "American" and "existentialism" were linked in the United States. Rice contemplated an American existentialism because he agreed with White's observation that existentialism might still be criticized but it could no longer be ignored. Rice contended that existentialism reminded American philosophers that they needed to probe further into the realm of human existence, that they should not rest until they provided a much more explicit description of the individual experience of existence. To make colleagues more comfortable with an existentialist perspective, however, Rice argued that human existence would have to be explored from an American vantage point, "not because we are chauvinists but because we are here rather than someplace else."[64]

Rice explored what an American perspective might entail by isolating existentialist doctrines and moods that resonated loudly in the United States. He found that the social and cultural context of anguish, freedom, and responsibility that helped fuel Sartreanism in the 1940s in France was a state with which Americans could more easily relate to in the mid-1950s. The postwar period had burdened the United States with the role of international power broker, and the country's global personification of political freedom encouraged Sartreanism's appeal to Americans, but the philosophy would also have to take on some different tonalities to gain a large following.

Absurdity and despair needed de-emphasis, Rice believed. American existentialism should instead "cling to as much meliorism as is compatible with recognizing that in some situations we have to invoke the tragic sense of life," Rice stated in his presidential address to the American Philosophical Association.[65] Rice observed that most Americans were not so naive as to believe in the total perfectibility of the individual, but he felt they did continue to adhere to a tempered faith in human progress. An American existentialism would have to incorporate the opinion that honest thought and diligence could do much to remove social and political evils.

Rice offered a detailed explanation of how existentialism might be modified to appeal to an American audience. It would have to be enlightened by "a scientific hypothesis that works" and should highlight the importance of an "extension of the self accompanied by a machinery obedient to human needs." An American existentialism should also recognize the necessity of settling political conflicts by the democratic process and should be religious in the sense of being "permeated with ultimate concern." To cap off all these requirements Rice added one more—the inclusion of a logical analysis of the meaning of the words "to be"![66] It was this final request in Rice's address that was most telling; if an outspoken advocate of existentialism in America noted the validity of the British logician Alfred Ayer's charge in 1945 that Sartre's use of "to be" lacked a logical framework, it was clear that any American existentialism would be so modified as to scarcely deserve the name.

Although some of the existentialist precepts in Sartreanism were taking firmer root because they filled in perceptual and methodological gaps in philosophical discourse and challenged the threat of the hegemony of empirical and analytic thought, these advances must be distinguished from philosophers' attitudes about Sartreanism as a unique strain of existentialism. Sartre's personal image did not make it easy for American philosophers to embrace his version of existentialism; his zealousness, atheism, opposition to the bourgeoisie, anti-anticommunism, political activism, and unacademic philosophizing were all qualities that disturbed many American philosophers.

Individuals both sympathetic and antagonistic toward Sartre commented on the negative impact of Sartre's personality and actions in their evaluation of his thought. As Brand Blanshard, a Yale philosophy professor and the dean of rationalism, later wrote: "I do not think his [Sartre's] thought carries much conviction to American philosophers, partly because of his abrasive personality which at times seems scarcely sane." And even Barnes, Sartre's translator and one of the first American philosophers to commit herself to existentialism, commented that in terms of personality alone, she preferred Camus.[67] The source of the opposition to Sartreanism cannot be tidily separated into philosophical and nonphilosophical reasons, but obviously the general response to Sartreanism was negatively affected by this tendency to find fault with Sartre's demeanor and behavior.

In conclusion, Sartreanism pulled philosophers in different directions during this middle stage of its American evolution. Some of its philosophical perspectives were better received than ever before, but Sartre's image and actions continued to have a harmful effect. Although the small number of American philosophers who were committed to a Sartrean viewpoint continued to grow, Sartre was at best a thorn in the sides of most—a needler of their consciences. He reminded them that human existence was complex, paradoxical, and deserving of much additional scrutiny. His outspokenness about the ills he perceived in the world around him warned more than one philosopher that they might have overly circumscribed their philosophical vision and reined in their personal involvement in politics, society, and culture too tightly.

5

An American Orientation, 1957–1963

The final stage in which American philosophers evaluated Sartreanism primarily as a philosophy of radical individualism rather than as a blend of existentialism and Marxism occurred after the publication of *Being and Nothingness* and before Barnes's translation of *Search for a Method* in 1963. Once again the limited accessibility of English versions of all of Sartre's philosophical works helped determine the content and chronology of the American discussion. Many philosophers were still largely unaware of the efforts Sartre had made since the early 1950s to integrate existentialism and Marxism and to develop the social ramifications of his philosophy. *Search for a Method* brought to a close a seventeen-year period in which early Sartreanism—considered as a philosophy of radical individualism—met and mingled with the plurality of currents within the American philosophical community.

During these years courses on Sartreanism sprouted on college campuses, the American Philosophical Association sponsored more symposia and sessions on the topic, and two of Sartre's earliest philosophical studies were translated. The Society for Phenomenology and Existential Philosophy, founded in 1962, signaled the school's growing importance within the circle of American philosophy by the end of this phase of early Sartreanism's evolution. This was also an era of considerable reflection on the philosophical significance of existentialism; more American philosophers were ready to assess the long-term impact of existentialism in general and of Sartreanism in particular after seventeen years of contact.

Sartreanism continued to bring structural changes to college philosophy departments in the late 1950s and early 1960s. The broad sweep of existentialism was covered as part of innumerable survey courses on Continental and contemporary philosophy, but classes that focused primarily on Sartreanism were added too. As we shall see, the rise in total undergraduate enrollment and graduate students in philosophy encouraged these courses because students felt a strong attraction to Sartreanism.[1]

The course lists at Columbia, Harvard, Yale, Princeton, and the University of Chicago—five of the nation's largest and most prestigious philosophy departments—pinpointed 1956 as the year that witnessed a significant increase in classes on Sartreanism, no doubt partly due to the new availability of *Being and Nothingness*. Kaelin, later a professor at Florida State University who made Sartrean aesthetics his special field in the late 1950s, remembered the difficulty of explaining Sartre without the aid of key translations: "I began teaching existentialism at Wisconsin [the University of Wisconsin, Madison, in 1955] at the urging of several of my colleagues. The chore became much easier when Hazel Barnes's translation of *Being and Nothingness* was published . . . her translation was probably the most influential event in determining Sartre's influence on a generation or two of students."[2]

More courses on existentialism and Sartreanism continued to be added in the following years. The professors who lobbied to get these classes into the curriculum were often already instrumental in bringing Sartre's ideas to the attention of colleagues and students through their written commentary. Kaufmann at Princeton launched "Hegel, Nietzsche, and Existentialism," a course that explored the two German philosophers' contributions to that philosophical school, after his *Existentialism from Dostoevsky to Sartre* virtually had become required reading in classes that covered contemporary philosophy. Schrader, the Kant scholar who became increasingly interested in Continental thought, discussed Sartre and Heidegger in the late 1950s in a new course at Yale entitled "Existential Philosophy."[3]

Wild eagerly added new classes on existentialism and phenomenology to the Harvard curriculum after a 1957 European sabbatical convinced him of the value of these schools. Wild offered a seminar in 1958 that compared phenomenology and linguistic analysis and helped bring Earle, the Northwestern philosopher who was a strong advocate of Continental thought, to Harvard as a visiting scholar. Earle, who studied existentialism and phenomenology under Gaston Berger at the University of Aix, taught a class entitled "European Existentialism" and a seminar that clarified Hegel's contribution.[4] Wild added two more courses in the same year—"European Existentialism and Pragmatism" and "Philosophical Anthropology."[5] The first course underscored the depth of Wild's interest in integrating the different currents of American and European philosophy.

Just as the number of college courses increased, so did symposia and sessions conducted by the American Philosophical Association. Only one major symposium was held prior to 1957, but two symposia and one session were offered in the years between 1957 and 1963. The Western Division of the American Philosophical Association conducted a symposium on existentialism and phenomenology at its annual meeting in 1959 at Madison, Wisconsin. The Eastern Division held a session in 1961 at Atlantic City, and in 1962 the Eastern Division presented another symposium entitled "Can we Dispense with Existence?" at its annual gathering in New York City.[6] Participants in these discussions were often familiar figures in the effort to inform the philosophical community about Sartreanism and existentialism. Barnes, Barrett, Cumming, Desan, Earle, Natanson, and Schrader were among the willing voices.

But the holding of symposia and sessions and audience receptivity were two different things. The Pacific Division and the Western (now Central) Division demonstrated more sympathy to Continental thought in all its variations than did the Eastern Division in these years. Kaelin at Florida State University recalled that the 1962 founding of the Society for Phenomenology and Existential Philosophy was a response to the belief that those schools could not receive a fair hearing within the American Philosophical Association because of its domination by the largely unsympathetic Eastern Division.[7]

The addresses of the presidents of the three sections in the late 1950s and early 1960s validated that perception. Three of the six speeches of the presidents of both the Pacific and Western Divisions were at least appreciative of the metaphysical and methodological contributions of existentialism, if not of all the specific tenets of Sartreanism. The only presidential address that lauded Continental thought in the Eastern Division was Wild's declaration of the importance of adopting an existentialist phenomenology, and many members reacted negatively to it. Anna-Teresa Tymieniecka, then a fellow at the Radcliffe Institute for Independent Studies and later the founder of the World Institute for Advanced Phenomenological Research and Learning, remembered:

> Wild's presidential lecture on the phenomenology of the life-world at the American Philosophical Association, Eastern Division, was by no means one that gave credit to this philosophy. Sidney Hook, a representative of one of the naturalistic trends of thought in the United States, approached me after it, asking in the most disparaging terms whether that loose talk was what I had always in our discussions claimed to be "First philosophy."[8]

Although the reception to existentialism varied greatly, the number of articles on Sartreanism proliferated in the middle of the 1950s and maintained its level of growth in the years that followed. The *Journal of Philosophy* continued to take the lead in the publication of Sartrean criticism. No doubt the journal transcended its naturalistic origins due to the presence of editors who were at least willing to give Sartreanism a hearing. Herbert Schneider and John Randall were rigorous critics, but they supported controversial discussion. Cumming, another Columbia professor who was also on the editorial board, was a staunch supporter of Sartre's ideas. The *Journal of Philosophy*'s new policy of publishing translations of excerpts from contemporary European philosophers, introduced in 1957, indicated the readiness to provide a forum. Noting that "the selections have been made with a view to the interests of American readers," the editors initiated the program by choosing selections from French philosophers because of the high American demand.[9] Two short excerpts from Sartre were among the first offerings.

The attitude of the *Journal of Philosophy*'s editors was important because the journal had the greatest readership among American philosophers. Next in line was the *Philosophical Review,* followed by the *Review of Metaphysics* and *Philosophy and Phenomenological Research.*[10]

The *Philosophical Review* published few articles on Sartreanism because it was primarily a forum for analytic philosophy, but the *Review of Metaphysics,* with its focus on speculative thought, and *Philosophy and Phenomenological Research,* because of its phenomenological bent, created opportunities for those involved in Continental thought to publish their work. *Philosophy and Phenomenological Research*'s emergence as one of the four most widely read journals in these years affirmed a rising interest in philosophical strands connected to Sartreanism.

Along with the *Journal of Philosophy*'s policy of providing excerpts in English, the course of Sartreanism's translation history took another positive turn. Forrest Williams and Robert Kirkpatrick collaborated to bring Sartre's theory of human consciousness to the attention of their colleagues via *The Transcendence of the Ego: An Existentialist Theory of Consciousness* (1957). That translation would offer philosophers who could not read French an opportunity to investigate the origins of Sartrean thought.[11] Williams was a former Fulbright fellow at the University of Paris and a colleague of Barnes at the University of Colorado. Kirkpatrick, who studied philosophy at Northwestern and came under the influence of Earle, was then a member of the Government Affairs Institute in Washington, D.C. Originally published in 1936, *The Transcendence of the Ego* established the parameters of most of the positions Sartre later developed in *Being and Nothingness.*

Williams and Kirkpatrick translated *The Transcendence of the Ego* largely as a labor of love rather than as a response to a loud clamoring for an English edition. They knew that the limited availability of Sartre's work in English diminished American philosophers' appreciation of the intricacies of Sartre's thought, and they wanted to correct that problem. Kirkpatrick initiated the project and then solicited Williams's help because of Williams's proficiency in French. Together they reworked Kirkpatrick's first draft and completed the new text in 1957.

Williams's involvement in translating Sartre both extended further back in the past and continued into the future. Williams's contact with Earle as a graduate student at Northwestern redirected his philosophical inquiries toward existentialism. The opportunity to study existentialism in France as a Fulbright fellow played a very significant role in his continuing interest in Continental thought, as it did with Columbia University philosophers Danto and others who reaped the benefits of this postwar scholarship foundation. While Williams was attending the University of Paris, he worked closely with Wahl, the first French philosophical ambassador of existentialism to teach at American universities in the mid-1940s.[12]

Wahl urged Williams to translate *L'Être et le néant* while Williams was still settling into his new responsibilities as a philosophy professor at the University of Colorado in the early 1950s. One day, Williams stopped by Barnes's office on the floor above him and was astonished to find her hard at work translating *L'Être et le néant*. Much relieved not to have to add this giant project to his list, he offered his opinion when requested, and Barnes continued her arduous job. Later, he did take on other translation tasks; *Imagination: A Psychological Critique* appeared after *The Transcendence of the Ego* in 1962 and offered more American philosophers an opportunity to weigh Sartre's opposition to contemporary theories of the imagination and to evaluate his phenomenological approach.[13] The publication both of *The Transcendence of the Ego* and of *Imagination* reflected sensitivity to the need to make the early roots of Sartreanism available for other philosophers' evaluation.

Book-length commentary also expanded in this phase of early Sartreanism's American experience, an expected consequence of the rising tide of interest. One tendency in this literature was an ongoing effort to reflect on Sartreanism within the context of the existentialist movement as a whole. Important overviews included Barrett's *Irrational Man: A Study in Existentialist Philosophy* (1958) and Robert Olson's *An Introduction to Existentialism* (1962). Barrett aimed for an audience that extended beyond professional philosophers, and *Irrational Man* became a "bestseller" in its field. Barrett explored not only the historical context of existentialism but its sociological significance as well. Olson's more academic work discussed existentialism's roots in the history of philosophy and the critical response of opposing schools. Publishers also capitalized on this market for overviews in 1959 when they reissued Grene's *Dreadful Freedom* (1948) as *An Introduction to Existentialism* without textual change. The Philosophical Library's decision to offer *A Concise Dictionary of Existentialism* in 1960 also spoke to a mounting interest in understanding the historical roots and meanings of the philosophy's terminology.[14]

* * *

By 1957 twelve years had passed since Sartreanism first began to attract philosophical notice in America. More philosophers were now familiar enough with Sartreanism to make more rigorous and detailed comparisons with other schools. They were especially eager to sort out the threads of continuity and differences between existentialism, phenomenology, the analytic movement, and pragmatism. Sartreanism's relationship to phenomenology became a particularly hotly debated topic. The motivation behind this flurry of interest in Sartreanism's connection to phenomenology was essentially evaluative; philosophers compared the two to assess strengths and weaknesses in both strands.[15] The interest in distinguishing the phenomenological from the existentialist elements in Sartre's approach was also a function of the process of specialization in American philosophy—the ongoing professional drive to separate philosophical structures analytically into their constitutive parts.

The history of existentialism's and phenomenology's association involved confusion in America as it did in France. Too often philosophers believed that the two were necessary partners.[16] The increasing tendency of American philosophers to identify Sartre as a "phenomenological existentialist" and to contrast him to "traditional existentialists" such as Kierkegaard and Nietzsche expressed a growing awareness of Sartre's special characteristics and his unique niche in the history of philosophy.

The symposium on phenomenology and existentialism arranged by the Western Division of the American Philosophical Association for its annual meeting in Madison, Wisconsin, on 30 April 1959 revealed the fundamental philosophical issues and high emotions that surrounded any discussion of Sartreanism. Herbert Spiegelberg, a nationally recognized expert on phenomenology, delivered a paper entitled "Husserl's Phenomenology and Existentialism" on the eve of publishing *The Phenomenological Movement: An Historical Introduction,* the first detailed historical account of this philosophical current in English. Earle, the Northwestern partisan of existentialism, presented "Phenomenology and Existentialism," and Natanson, the Sartre scholar who was then teaching at the University of North Carolina, closed the symposium with "Phenomenology and Existentialism: Husserl and Sartre on Intentionality."[17] Following the time-honored format, Spiegelberg and Earle presented opposing views in the debate over existentialism's relation to phenomenology, and Natanson suggested a possible reconciliation.

The heart of the controversy was whether or not existentialism should dominate phenomenology and be regarded as the superior school with the more important agenda. As a Husserl scholar, Spiegelberg resented existentialism's popularity: "To be sure, Husserl's new fame in this country shines largely with a reflective light. Its source is the still fashionable interest in the child of the strange alliance between Kierkegaard's 'unscientific' existential thinking and Husserl's new phenomenological science that goes by the name of existentialism." Spiegelberg's specific target was Sartreanism. He was disgruntled that although this French school had essential roots in Husserlian phenomenology, it was Sartreanism that received the limelight. He rightfully protested the tendency to read flaws in Sartreanism as flaws in phenomenology. The Lawrence College professor criticized Sartre for bastardizing the phenomenological method by selectively emphasizing isolated aspects of an approach that was broadly conceived and for minimizing a scientific bent that involved searching for coherent propositions designed to eliminate restrictive presuppositions.[18]

Spiegelberg conceded that existentialism might be pursuing more vital contemporary interests than was pure phenomenology because it focused on the currently popular topic of human existence, but he faulted existentialists for failing to observe the philosophical principles of solidity, integrity, and humility. Spiegelberg had Sartre in mind when he invoked Husserl's warning to philosophers that "one needs bright ideas, but one must not publish them" and "one must not consider oneself too good to work on the foundations." These complaints echoed the ongoing negative observations that Sartre was too inclined to showy displays of creative genius and that he needed to shore up his ethical and epistemological foundations. Spiegelberg concluded with the acerbic comment: "It would indeed be a betrayal of the spirit of Husserl's philosophizing if phenomenology should sell its birthright for a mess of existentialist pottage."[19]

Earle strongly disagreed with Spiegelberg's position. What Spiegelberg really wanted, Earle argued, was "a phenomenological existentialism, with phenomenology keeping the whip hand." The Northwestern professor insisted that the worst possible course for existentialism was to pattern itself meekly after the more rational contours of phenomenology. Existentialism and phenomenology, he contended, were incompatible movements; the more existentialists like Sartre tried to embrace the rational techniques of phenomenology, the more existentialism was inclined to lose sight of its reason for being—the investigation of "existence itself, passion, decision, life, vitality, and self-affirmation."[20]

Philosophers like Sartre, who tried to incorporate phenomenology into the older tradition of existentialism expressed in Kierkegaard and Nietzsche, Earle believed, got themselves into trouble precisely because they attempted to blend the passion of existence with the more rational truths pursued by phenomenologists. Earle vigorously maintained that existence could not be described like any other phenomenon and that phenomenological existentialists went against the most basic principle of existentialism—that there were no essential doctrines or methods whatsoever. He concluded by pointing out that if the use of phenomenological approaches should produce consensus on the nature of existence because of their rational structure, their value was disproved because there was no uncontestable agreement. And Earle found the disagreement extremely positive because it showed him that instead of presenting phenomenological ontologies of human existence, philosophers like Sartre were really offering ontological autobiographies in which they analyzed their own personal choices in their unique existences. For Earle, this was exactly as it should be, because "the properly philosophical task is not to boil it [existence] all down to a common doctrine, but rather to deepen our sense of the uniqueness, of what is happily, its irreplaceability, its undeducibility."[21]

Natanson sympathized with the resounding complaints of Husserl scholars like Spiegelberg, but he also agreed with Earle's passionate belief that existentialism was not the "mess of pottage" that Spiegelberg made it out to be. In his concluding paper Natanson underscored the point that there could be no question that Sartrean existentialism was profoundly indebted to Husserlian phenomenology. He also noted that Sartre modified Husserl's method by rejecting the process of phenomenological reduction and Husserl's view of the function of the individual ego. Natanson agreed with Spiegelberg and others that the grounds on which Sartre rejected some of Husserl's conclusions were shaky, and that Sartre's flaws were not necessarily Husserl's too.[22]

Natanson, however, joined Earle in finding great value in existentialism's revelation of irreducible existence. Natanson's intent in this mediation was to break down the dichotomous view of existentialism as a sloppy, frivolous, and evanescent philosophy and phenomenology as a respectable, serious school unfairly injured by its association with existentialism. And, unlike Spiegelberg or Earle, Natanson found no grave sin in Sartre's effort to combine the two—together they might create a productive synthesis.[23] The exchange between these philosophers illustrated not only the strong feelings attached to any discussion of existentialism but also the eagerness to clarify the purpose that existentialism might serve in the pursuit of philosophical knowledge.

Philosophers continued to probe the relation between existentialism and analytic thought in the late 1950s and early 1960s. Barrett laid out the reigning view of analytic philosophers' perception of existentialism in the last pages of *Irrational Man:* the "existence" of existential philosophy was not a legitimate concept because, in the Kantian sense, it did not logically bind together mental images that were ultimately derived from sensory data. Barrett complained in particular that many American philosophers who stuck fast to such logical and empirical traditions were basically unable to see the forest for the trees; in denying the importance of the existentialists' concept of existence because it was cloudy, they ignored the fact that existence was the contextual ground in which more logical structures were formulated. Barrett pointed out that when philosophers "logicized" they tended to forget existence, but "they must first exist in order to logicize."[24]

On a more positive note, Barrett also discerned continued glimmerings of signs that philosophers were now paying more attention to the possibility of accepting the Kantian construction of a valid concept but putting it to a different use. Instead of relying on Kant to undermine the legitimacy of existentialism's presentation of existence, they could follow Kierkegaard's path and inquire into existence precisely because it transcended Kant's definition of a concept; existence would not be meaningless because it was too empty and thin but would be more meaningful because it was too rich and dense to be defined fully by discrete sensory data.

Here Barrett observed the expansion of philosophical bridges under construction between existentialism and analytic thought. In the late 1950s and early 1960s, some philosophers pursued the connections between the study of analytic philosophy and Continental inquiry that people like White and Hendel noted earlier. Hans Meyerhoff, a German-born philosopher at the University of California, Los Angeles, who immigrated in 1934 to escape Nazism, observed in the *Chicago Review* article "The Return to the Concrete" that the phenomenological reflection on the things themselves "has occurred in recent English philosophy, only under a different label, for the 'ordinary things' across the channel are words and sentences rather than the totality of existence."[25] Ordinary language philosophy, argued Meyerhoff, was nothing but phenomenology in disguise. Meyerhoff was a Plato scholar, but he was also keenly interested in existentialism and the philosophy of history and taught all three topics at UCLA. His most fundamental interest was in the human condition, and his integration of philosophy, history, and literature meshed perfectly with existentialist methodologies.

But not all philosophers were as amenable as Meyerhoff to drawing parallels between analytic philosophy and Continental thought. Wild's personal journey revealed some of the other characteristics of the relationship between existentialism and analytic thought in the American philosophical landscape in the late 1950s and early 1960s. Wild was never a staunch advocate of Sartreanism, but the problems and possibilities that he encountered provide a window on Sartreanism's fate.

Wild began his career as a realist unconcerned with Continental philosophy, but he became avidly interested in it in the late 1950s. He spent a sabbatical year at the Husserl Archives in Louvain in 1957, and when he returned to Harvard he was committed to the idea of spreading an existentialist-minded phenomenology throughout America. Tymieniecka, a leader in the movement to make Americans cognizant of phenomenology, attended a gathering at the home of Harvard philosophy professor George Burch in which Wild reported on the outcome of his sabbatical. Tymieniecka remembered: "To my enormous surprise . . . I heard an enthusiastic proclamation of phenomenology as the philosophy of our age and of his decision to spread it in the United States by all possible means."[26] Acting on this commitment, Wild aggressively added courses on existentialism and phenomenology to the Harvard curriculum.

Wild's project of popularizing existentialism and phenomenology in America led him to the unprecedented step of becoming the first member of the Harvard philosophy department ever to leave because of philosophical incompatibility. That action provides a sense of the fervor that Continental thought was able to impart in some of the key figures in the American movement. Wild resigned from Harvard in 1960 convinced that his mission to spread an existential phenomenology was doomed at Cambridge. An anonymous reporter discussed Wild's departure in an article that was published in the *Harvard Crimson,* the undergraduate student newspaper. Wild's decision, the reporter observed, was the result of "certain contemporary philosophical tendencies which he felt had come to dominate the Harvard Philosophy Department of the time to such an extent as to treat other, presumably more humanistic tendencies, as contemptible."[27] Wild felt isolated at Harvard because philosophical thought there was centered on substantive proofs and mathematic theory; the faculty also had recently voted to hire two more logicians. Wild hoped his new post as chair of Northwestern's philosophy department would give him an opportunity to build a department that would become a center for existential and phenomenological philosophy in the United States.[28]

Comments made by analytically minded faculty members revealed the unsupportive environment Wild encountered at Harvard. Quine, a logician whose pathbreaking work gained him an international reputation, acknowledged that Wild's resignation would leave a large gap, but he expressed the view that the department would be better off if it put its money and energy into filling that hole with more logic. Donald C. Williams, a logician who also taught courses on traditional metaphysics, contended that the Harvard philosophy department was losing its preeminence because it had not followed the example of other prestigious universities and tightened its focus on the new methods of logic and philosophical analysis.[29]

Wild's stay at Northwestern lasted less than two years. After Paul Weiss learned that Wild would be willing to move, he encouraged Wild to join him at Yale. Weiss remembered that when Wild arrived "the department took him to its bosom" because Blanshard, Hendel, Schrader, and Weiss all encouraged the serious consideration of many strands of speculative thought.[30] Wild's personal journey mirrored the reception of Sartreanism in two ways; just as Wild met with strong opposition at Harvard, Sartreanism encountered powerful foes in the academic community. Ultimately, however, Wild found a safe haven for his interests at Yale, just as Sartreanism, too, found institutions where it would be nurtured.

The farthest reach of Sartreanism's Americanization was its identification with the pragmatism of William James. Philosophers frequently noted similarities in the acceptance of an open and contingent universe and a broadly conceived empiricism that acknowledged emotions, as well as sense experiences, as data.[31] Barrett, for example, wondered in *Irrational Man* whether it would not be more accurate to call James an existentialist rather than a pragmatist. Barrett explained that the Jamesian characteristics that often embarrassed contemporary pragmatists—the personal tone of James's philosophizing, his willingness to give psychology the final word over logic—were part of the bedrock of existentialism.[32] Philosophers like Barnes and Meyerhoff listed the broad congruities between existentialism and radical empiricism. Both schools rejected a block universe encased in a rational structure. Both were also realist philosophies, again in the widest sense; James and the existentialists opposed an overemphasis on the mind's role in creating a reality.[33]

Existentialism and pragmatism were grounded in the movement toward the concrete that got under way at the turn of the century; their practitioners hoped to take philosophy away from the realm of abstraction. Pragmatists and existentialists agreed that "existence precedes essence" and asked how individuals constructed reality through meanings and values. Both focused on human problems in the world and emphasized the need for individual action to resolve these issues. "Truth" was relative, always conditioned by the limitations imposed by partial knowledge.[34]

But no matter how many points of convergence were unearthed, philosophers never confused existentialism and Jamesian pragmatism; critical distinctions appeared in epistemology, individual existence, mood, and theory of value. James, like other pragmatists, adopted an experimental theory of knowledge; every true statement depended upon the outcome of an experiment of some kind in the world. That experiment was not always overtly "scientific," but it did involve the intelligent use of logic and observation. The pragmatic theory of truth was essentially an extension of the logic and values of scientific inquiry.[35] The structure surrounding individual existence was different too. Existentialists and pragmatists made the human being the point of philosophical departure, but pragmatists were much more inclined to observe people as biological organisms responding to the totality of their environments with the intent of using those environments advantageously.

And pragmatists were simply more optimistic. Although they recognized the power and prevalence of the tragic sense of life, their view was fundamentally cheerful. In "Existentialism in America," a lecture presented to visiting French Fulbright scholars in 1960, Barnes expressed the difference to humorous perfection. The pragmatist "always seems to be just coming out of his cold shower, full of exuberance," quipped Barnes, "while the existentialist is more likely to be hovering at the bridge wondering whether or not to jump." Barrett carried the contrast even further. The difference between John Dewey and the existentialists, claimed Barrett, "is the difference between America and Europe"; pragmatism still expressed America's optimism about the possibility of technological and scientific mastery over nature, while existentialism reflected Europe's disillusionment.[36]

Finally, ethical theories in existentialism and pragmatism were oppositional. Hook argued strenuously that the existentialists' moral philosophy was "inadequate and viciously inadequate, because of its glorification of the arbitrary and irrational."[37] He maintained that the existentialists established no basis for responsible moral action because one value seemed to be as good as any other. Hook echoed the ongoing complaint that Sartre, in particular, universalized the logic of extreme situations by turning moral contexts that required choice into extreme episodes necessitating desperate measures. Hook's chief complaint boiled down to his perception that existentialism paid little attention to the importance of relying on rational intelligence to formulate a responsible and moral plan of action.

* * *

Philosophers' discussions of Sartreanism's connections with other disciplines in the late 1950s and early 1960s were a natural product of the interdisciplinary core that lay at the heart of Sartre's thought; his ideas and categories wove together the insights of literature, psychology, psychoanalysis, art, and philosophy. But the attention philosophers paid to interdisciplinary applications also suggested a search to find a new niche for philosophy for those who felt it had lost its preeminence as the academy's fountain of knowledge. In "The Return to the Concrete," Meyerhoff at UCLA considered the current interest in the interconnections between philosophy and literature as an expression of philosophy's need to find a new reason for being. "Philosophy is in bad shape," Meyerhoff lamented, "in part for want of identity." Philosophy's traditional enterprise—investigating the nature of being—nearly suffered a deathblow from members of the analytic school who found such inquiries meaningless and from the proliferation of sciences that defined their own realms of existence, Meyerhoff observed. Literature, however, provided a new source of identity for philosophy because it connected with the philosophical movement to return to the concrete that now surfaced in schools such as existentialism.[38]

The central idea shared by literature and existentialism, said Meyerhoff, was that poetry was more true than philosophy; traditional philosophy did not take adequate note of the range of human experience or the significance of irrational and unconscious ways of being. While Meyerhoff was quick to establish that he did not believe "this return to the concrete is the whole of philosophy," he very much appreciated both the energy it gave to contemporary philosophy and its interest in direct empirical observation of existence rather than in too rarefied abstraction. Meyerhoff was struck by the link between this last quality and the venerable American tradition of paying attention to everyday experience.[39]

Meyerhoff posed the fundamental question: Is there lasting value in a philosophy like Sartreanism that operates on the principle that literature holds truths missed by traditional philosophy? A philosophy that adopts literary methods, responded Meyerhoff with deep conviction, was valuable precisely because it explored the world people lived in: "It tells us something worth knowing—even though these poetic truths may not be very respectable when judged by the strict etiquette of scientific knowledge."[40]

Interest in Sartreanism's connections with literature was not only the expression of philosophy's desire to find a new niche, as Meyerhoff suggested, but also the result of the ongoing development of the field of aesthetics within the discipline. Aesthetics became an increasingly sophisticated and respected specialty within the profession after its earlier growth spurt in the 1940s, and this had positive consequences for Sartreanism as one of the few philosophical currents to employ literature as an avenue of knowledge. Barnes's *The Literature of Possibility: A Study in Humanistic Existentialism* (1959) reflected this interest in aesthetics and literature as a philosophical medium.[41]

Some American philosophers were now more willing to entertain the idea that the philosopher who spoke through literature might gain certain advantages; these could include vividness and dramatic intensity in the presentation of moral issues, the capability of recreating emotions and sensations, and the opportunity of thoroughly engaging the reader. One of the unstated messages contained in the *Journal of Philosophy*'s decision to publish translated excerpts from Sartre's literary works was this greater openness to philosophy's association with literature.

The exploration of Sartreanism's interdisciplinary nature also extended to psychiatry and psychology. The publication of *Existence: A New Dimension in Psychiatry and Psychology* in 1958 and the coverage of existential psychiatry in popular magazines helped spur interest. Meyerhoff predicted in "The Return to the Concrete" that "the new hit called 'existential analysis' which is now being imported into this country with considerable éclat . . . will undoubtedly be a success because even *Time* magazine is promoting it."[42] Editors Rollo May, Ernest Angel, and Henri Ellenberger collaborated for four years to bring together *Existence,* a collection of essays that explained the origin and therapeutic application of the existential movement in psychoanalysis. May, an American psychoanalyst whose interest in existentialism was rooted in the psychological insights of Jaspers and Heidegger, worked closely with Ellenberger, a Swiss psychotherapist with extensive clinical experience in existential psychiatry, to make a bridge between existential theories and American psychotherapy. Angel, another Swiss psychotherapist, originated the project and bore the brunt of translation.[43]

Philosophers' considerations of Sartre's investigations of the human psyche focused on a comparison of the metaphysical and empirical underpinnings of Freudian and Sartrean psychoanalysis, the experimental stage of Sartre's hypothesis, and its possible therapeutic benefits. A debate between Schrader at Yale and Harry Tiebout at the University of Illinois, Urbana, suggested that there was little difficulty in agreeing that Sartre's concepts were only a sketchy framework for an applied psychology that did not yet offer a proven therapy. Disagreement between Schrader and Tiebout flared over the wisdom of blending existentialist metaphysics with any form of psychoanalysis.

Schrader worried in "Existential Psychoanalysis and Metaphysics," an article published in 1959 in the *Review of Metaphysics,* that it would be unwise to set up psychoanalysis with an existentialist ontology in which individuals transcended a causal network of scientific facts because of their ability to choose. He argued that psychoanalysis should follow in Freud's footsteps and try to preserve its metaphysical autonomy as a scientific discipline. Tiebout, who taught courses in religion and theology and who became interested in existentialism due to the influence of Tillich, disagreed in his article "Tillich, Existentialism, and Psychoanalysis," published in the *Journal of Philosophy* that same year. Tiebout maintained that although Freud tried to make psychiatry a science in the narrow sense and perceived the human psyche in mechanistic terms, he ultimately fell back on an existentialist ontology. Tiebout saw no real conflict between the metaphysical substratum of existential psychiatry and Freudian psychoanalysis; although Freud tried to force the psyche into a rigid model, his case studies always revealed the irreducibility of human freedom and choice.[44] This debate over the proper relationship between ontology and psychotherapy, however, was not taken up by many other philosophers; the majority were still willing to leave the field of Sartrean psychoanalysis to psychiatric professionals.

* * *

Along with interdisciplinary connections, philosophers also took particular notice of Sartreanism's ethical arguments in the late 1950s and early 1960s. Many philosophers' perspectives on Sartrean morality had changed considerably since the early years of introduction; no one described this morality as frighteningly nihilistic now, as had happened frequently in the beginning. Sartrean ethics was more often characterized as humanistic. For some American philosophers, Sartreanism managed to complete an ethical journey from nihilism to existential humanism in less than two decades.

Philosophers often approved of the relativistic tone of Sartrean morality but still had reservations about the weight Sartre gave to the individual's role in making ethical decisions. In short, many approved of Sartre's step away from absolute values but did not feel that an overly subjective morality was a suitable replacement. Paul Kurtz, who made value theory one of his special concerns while teaching at Union College in Nebraska, noted the positive and negative aspects of Sartre's moral relativism. In "Kierkegaard, Existentialism, and the Contemporary Scene," an article published in the *Antioch Review* in 1961, Kurtz stated: "The existentialists are saying something important, I submit, when they point to the fact of human decision." He added, however, that "our choices are not purely subjective; nor need they be capricious or arbitrary."[45]

Along the same lines, in "Pragmatism and Existentialism" Hook praised the existentialists for recognizing that moral choices should be applauded as individual actions, but he sternly warned that the limitations of subjectivism needed to be guarded against. Hook created a memorable image to state his case: "We should welcome the existentialist's declaration that one must take a stand. But you can take a stand on your head or on your feet."[46]

Olson, a philosophy professor at Rutgers, was another one of those who was eager to sort out the virtues and flaws in Sartreanism in the late 1950s and early 1960s. One of Olson's chief objectives in writing *An*

Introduction to Existentialism in 1962 was to evaluate the strength of the existentialists' critique of ethical formulations in contemporary philosophy. Olson, like many other philosophers interested in existentialism, benefited from the renewed opportunity to do graduate work in French institutions after the war. He described the existentialists' moral stance as the substitution of the value of intensity and authenticity—manifested in acts of free choice—for the more traditional philosophical values of truth and human happiness. In particular, existentialists argued that the value of happiness was unattainable and therefore human existence was "a tragic condition."[47] The Rutgers philosophy professor observed that many American philosophers regarded the existentialists' rejection of values such as truth and happiness as a subjective decision determined by individual temperament and social conditioning. The existentialists could make the value of human freedom, for example, into an objective and universal ethic in the eyes of the majority of American philosophers only if they would employ scientific methodology and determine the frequency with which individuals acknowledged the worth of freedom. Then, using the principle of induction, the observed regularity could be postulated as a behavioral law.

Existentialists, of course, disdained this method and replied that they considered the value of freedom a fact of the human condition. That position brought them face to face with their own charge of absolutism. Alvin Plantinga, a philosopher of religion at Wayne State University who pioneered a rebirth of philosophical theology in the postwar era, spoke for many others when he concluded in "An Existentialist's Ethics," an article that appeared in the *Review of Metaphysics* in 1958: "If each of us lives in a world of his own choosing, then the world of absolute freedom which Sartre has chosen is rationally no more compelling than any other. . . . If Sartre is right, there is no reason to think that he is right."[48] In sum, Sartrean ethics never met the canons of verifiability and objectivity it consistently confronted in the American philosophical community. What did change was the greater recognition of the wisdom of setting the entire ethical discussion in a context of relativity rather than absolutism. Sartreanism helped pave the way for the wave of interest in "situational ethics" in the 1960s.

Assessments of Sartrean morality naturally included views on Sartre's political ethics. Here the theme of irrationality played an important role. Liberal-minded philosophers often read Sartre's political theory as an irrationalism unstructured by any logical political plan that might foster a better social order. Olson noted this inclination in *An Introduction to Existentialism:* "From almost all sides existentialism has been proclaimed a movement of irrationalism. Political liberals condemn the movement on this ground above all others." Kurtz was a case in point; in "Kierkegaard, Existentialism, and the Contemporary Scene," he too worried over the irrational overtones of existentialism's political theory. Marxism's sanguinity about the social future that the rational application of science and technology would usher in, Kurtz suspected, would have a wide appeal to underdeveloped countries. The existentialists' loss of faith in the rationalism of science and technology, he further feared, would be too appealing to disillusioned individuals in the West.[49]

A few philosophers evaluated Sartre's political ethics more positively. Barrett not only was undisturbed by any "irrational" threads in Sartrean political thought but was supportive of them if they translated into ideological opposition to the mechanistic assumptions of the Communist Party. Sartre, maintained Barrett, recognized inalienable subjectivity, while the party insisted upon an inevitable historical progression in which the individual was reduced to an object in an immutable process. Barrett singled out Sartre's political morality as the most valuable part of his philosophy. Sartre's self-appointed job as watchdog of individual rights in the midst of Marxism, Barrett insisted, "was the effort of a man of great good will, generosity and courage; and the project he has chosen as his own, in which he has chosen himself, is the humanitarian and liberal one of revolutionary action."[50]

Levi, the Washington University professor well known for his work on the social context of philosophy who wrote on Sartrean ontology in a 1956 *Ethics* article "A Quixotic Quest for Being," responded to the apprehensions of such philosophers as Kurtz in "The Meaning of Existentialism for Contemporary International Relations," a 1962 article in *Ethics.*[51] Levi acknowledged that existentialism was not as oriented toward the political future as was either Marxism or democratic liberalism, the former with its utopian goal of achieving solidarity through an alternative class structure, the latter with its plan to establish a political community through a scientifically engineered social reconstruction. Instead of worrying about whether the irrational overtones of existentialism would encourage people to withdraw from political activity because of a loss of faith in rational progress, however, Levi urged philosophers like Kurtz to see the ramifications of existentialism in a more positive light.

Taking Sartreanism as an example, Levi showed that existentialism's meaning for international relations involved a critical shift in perspective that made the individual the measure of political actions and asserted a new view of global conflicts; political issues were not primarily problems to be solved by the application of mechanistic theories of the social sciences but as inescapable conflicts within moral life. Existentialism's ability to align with a variety of ideologies, Levi concluded, should be positively interpreted as a sign that "there is no absolute contradiction of human interests, between Marxist and liberal democratic existentialism, perhaps between the Russians and ourselves." Levi believed existentialism suggested the possibility of a synthesis at a level deeper than political rhetoric.[52]

Just as political concerns stimulated philosophers' interest in Sartrean ethics, so did college students' attraction to the subject. Sartreanism captured the attention of the new generation of college students that came of age in the early 1960s. The rise in the number of courses that focused specifically on Sartreanism and more generally on existentialism owed much to this student interest. Sartreanism was a strong magnet for young people because its issues were their issues and its tone was the rebellious one of youth. Sartreanism's fundamental concerns— individual autonomy, responsibility, and authenticity—were the classic problems of college students struggling to define the limits of their freedom within the confines of family structure, campus life, and university bureaucracy.

Sartreanism asked the key question that young people often posed as they embarked on adult life: "What meaning does individual existence have?" And in answer, early Sartreanism emphasized a doctrine of radical individual liberty that presupposed no external authority to which young people had to bend the knee. In addition, Sartre asserted the responsibility attached to freedom and the meaning that came with the pursuit of one's own project. But many students forgot the emphasis on accountability and remembered only the cry for individual liberty and the insurgent tone. Jeff Mason, a transplanted American philosopher who later taught in England, recalled that in 1963 when he was a philosophy student at the University of California, Santa Barbara, Sartreanism was the intellectual plaything of "hip" students: "Ferlinghetti, Ginsberg, *On the Road* with Jack Kerouac. Coffee houses, a book store with chess sets (the Red Lion), folk music, marijuana. Equal parts of earnestness, zaniness, and questioning. Sartre's existentialism was part of the beatnik or 'proto-hippy' baggage which was de rigueur in a certain minority of arty and intellectual students."[53]

The negative side of these students' interest was that it sometimes did not go beyond the view that Sartreanism stood only for antiauthoritarianism. And Sartreanism's identification with the Beat movement—that literary school of cultural criticism that challenged the affluence and social conservatism of postwar middle-class existence—had negative consequences for some philosophy professors who equated it with undisciplined, unprincipled literary hooliganism. Olson revealed this damning connection in *An Introduction to Existentialism* by swiftly discrediting the Beat school as "a degenerate form of existentialism for the weak-minded and weak-willed products of American educational institutions."[54]

Archie Bahm, a philosophy professor at the University of New Mexico and the editor of *The Directory of American Philosophers,* underscored the theme. He saw a natural affinity between young people and existentialist thought because of the philosophy's supposed appeal to individuals seeking the freedom to gratify almost any desire. Bahm even rashly predicted that philosophies like Sartreanism that were attractive to youth "may be expected to flourish more, now that the average age of all U.S. citizens has been lowered to about 25." In sum, Bahm viewed Sartreanism as the perfect philosophy for what he perceived as a gratification-minded, irresponsible baby-boom generation. Bahm ruminated gloomily about the appeal of Sartreanism: "Now accustomed to instant coffee, etc., and expecting further progress toward 'instant women,' many somehow expect to find 'instant philosophy.' "[55]

But others were not so quick to write off their students' attraction to existentialism as an expression of arrested psychological development. Gray, chair of the Philosophy Department at Colorado College in the early 1960s and a scholar of German existentialism, acknowledged some of the shallower sources of existentialism's magnetism, but he also emphasized the more positive and substantive roots. Gray wove these factors together in a 1965 *Harper's* article, "Salvation on the Campus: Why Existentialism Is Capturing the Students."[56]

When Gray first began teaching his senior seminar "Freedom and Authority" in 1950, he observed that the interest in Sartre and other existentialists was largely owing to their novelty. Gray pointed out that Americans always were susceptible to philosophical imports from the Continent and England and added that any new currents had their own special appeal: "I must also admit rather shamefacedly, that even philosophy is not immune to the attraction of the 'hottest thing in town.'"[57] But Gray's close contact with his students in the "Freedom and Authority" seminar made it clear that for many students there was more to existentialism's appeal than notoriety, especially as Sartreanism lost its faddish veneer.

The heart of the matter, Gray believed, lay in young people's sincere attempts to grapple with the meaning of individual freedom and authenticity. The Colorado College professor drew on particular social and historical factors to explain Sartreanism's dynamism, including the new collegiate environment at the end of the 1950s and the beginning of the 1960s. Partly in response to the increased enrollment that the first wave of baby boomers brought, American colleges and universities were now becoming huge bureaucracies. College life was much more impersonal than it had been for earlier generations, and students sometimes felt reduced to their Social Security number. They complained about the difficulty of making personal contact with the administration, faculty, and even other students.

After listening to these expressions of alienation, Gray felt that young people were particularly susceptible to Sartre's urging to assert individual freedom in the midst of a crowd. He was also struck by the fact that many took seriously Sartre's insistence on the responsibilities attached to freedom. Gray noted that in earlier years causes that provided students with the opportunity to engage in responsible action had been more readily available. Fascism and World War II were rallying cries in the 1930s and 1940s, but by the 1950s such compelling issues were gone, and so young people often found Sartre's search for the meaning of individual existence especially pertinent. Students in the early 1960s, Gray pointed out, were just beginning to find causes that would assuage a sense of alienation and provide an outlet for responsible action when they protested racial segregation and university administrations' denial of student rights.[58]

Finally, Gray's observation of how students eagerly applied Sartrean ethics to their own sense of estrangement reinforced his own existentialist search for meaning as a philosopher. Gray found that meaning in intensifying his pedagogical efforts to help young people discover values on which to anchor authenticity and social activism. Gray recognized the danger that Sartreanism might be read solely as a call to escape authority and values, but he asked himself and his profession to encourage students to take the next step in Sartrean ethics—assume responsibility. Gray urged his colleagues not to "retreat into research, government contract, and sabbatical travel" but to renew the "cooperative search by teacher and taught for an authority upon which to base freedom and individuality."[59] The Colorado College philosopher's request underscored the generational component of Sartreanism's appeal; he counseled his peers to look beyond Sartre's emphasis on radical freedom in order to mend the rift between generations that youth's attraction to the French philosophy expressed.

* * *

The years after the translation of *Being and Nothingness* in 1956 and prior to the translation of *Search for a Method* in 1963 were ones in which important structural changes occurred in Sartreanism's American development. Student interest generated new courses, translations were more readily available, and a greater number of American philosophers became well schooled in Sartreanism. The capstone of these structural changes was the founding of the Society for Phenomenology and Existential Philosophy in 1962 at Northwestern University. Now philosophers who wanted to explore existentialism and phenomenology had a ready forum for their inquiries.

The chief instigator of the new society was John Wild. With a knack for organizing associations, Wild was dedicated to the idea of popularizing phenomenology in particular and existentialism too. Wild encouraged James Edie, his colleague at Northwestern, and Aron Gurwitsch, a leading phenomenologist at the New School for Social Research, to serve with him as officers of the new organization. The establishment of the Society for Phenomenology and Existential Philosophy fit well with Wild's mission to encourage the spread of an existentialist-minded phenomenology. Sartreanism benefited, too, because the group became a clearinghouse for any ideas that fell under the common denominator of its name.[60] Not until the Sartre Society of North America was founded in 1985, however, did Sartreanism have its own association.[61]

Shortly after the founding of the Society for Phenomenology and Existential Philosophy, Barnes's 1963 translation of *Search for a Method* signaled the end of Sartre's "early existentialist" period in American philosophy. Although Sartre's efforts to mix existentialism and Marxism began in the first half of the 1950s, the majority of American philosophers in these years continued to deal with Sartre's work chiefly as a unique expression of existentialism because the shorter pieces that wove in Marxism were not often translated or easily available in the original version. After *Search for a Method*, the primary question was whether existentialism and Marxism could be profitably blended rather than the validity of the concept of radical freedom.

In *Search for a Method*, Barnes included another comprehensive and extremely thoughtful introduction to Sartre's latest stance; she quickly brought to the foreground the key issues that Sartre's new offering presented. The University of Colorado professor pointed out that Sartre did not reduce human beings to their biological or economic function but reevaluated his conception of the relationship between the individual and society.[62] Critics on both the political Right and Left attacked the idea of radical freedom in *Being and Nothingness* because they claimed it put too little emphasis on biological and social conditioning. Sartre, opponents charged, offered no viable social or political theory; the individual was free but placed in an imaginary world devoid of real pressures ensuing from the existence of others. The new work represented Sartre's endeavor to merge existentialism and Marxism to create an integrated theory that could cope with a complex intersubjective world.

Another question now came into finer focus: Did Sartre betray the individualistic orientation of his early thought by incorporating Marxist theory? Barnes stated the concern of many American philosophers when they encountered *Search for a Method:* "How are we to place this new work? Who is this new Sartre?"[63] The stakes were very high; if Sartre could reconcile the subjective cast of his early work with Marxism's imperatives of social conditioning, he would fulfill the promise he made in *Being and Nothingness* to establish an ethics that would show how radically free beings could meaningfully commit themselves to values.

Although American philosophers who had read *Existentialism* and *Being and Nothingness* had already pondered the question of successfully blending Sartre's idea of freedom with the political and social limitations that Sartre acknowledged, the translation of *Search for a Method* raised the issue of mating existentialism and Marxism to a much more visible level. While the interpretive framework in which Sartre's works were considered had been primarily that of the super-structure of existentialist philosophy, by 1963 it was becoming one of existentialism and Marxism. The first major paradigm in which Sartrean thought was evaluated within the American philosophical community was transcended.

* * *

What were the major contours of early Sartreanism's seventeen-year journey in American philosophy? Because it was a movement that attracted people outside the world of academic philosophy, it brought into that world some issues that usually escaped philosophers' purview. Sartreanism prodded American philosophers to relinquish their vision of what philosophy "should be" and goaded them to think more about its social and political ramifications. Sartreanism's journey in America was also an interdisciplinary one. Because Sartreanism mingled the worlds of philosophy, literature, psychiatry, psychology, and politics, it helped build bridges between philosophy and these disciplines. Sartreanism was also a school that generated very strong reactions within the philosophical community; outspoken advocates argued that it was the only philosophy for the mid–twentieth century because it confronted the sense of spiritual and ideological crisis head-on; opponents ridiculed it as a frivolous blend of irrationalism and despair. Yet because such compelling issues as freedom, responsibility, and the limits of reason formed its thematic core, Sartreanism could not be easily ignored.

Early Sartreanism's evolution in America was forcefully shaped by its progression from a body of thought at first dismissed by many as faddish to a school considered worthy of investigation. This sequence of initial popularity outside the philosophical community and the normal ebbing of notoriety greatly affected the way some philosophers perceived Sartreanism. At first many passed over it without even giving it a thorough reading, but when the voguishness wore off they were at least more likely to investigate Sartreanism's concepts. Sartreanism entered with an important strike against it, but the natural evanescence of fads ultimately helped the philosophy to gain a more equitable hearing.

Sartreanism's progression from being dismissed as a literary school to being taken seriously as a philosophical movement was integrally linked to this evolution from a body of thought initially perceived as a caprice to one meriting serious consideration. Throughout the seventeen-year period many American philosophers wrestled with the propriety of linking literature and philosophy until, at the end, Sartreanism completed a successful transformation from a literary current to a philosophical movement in the eyes of most skeptics. This hurdle was a difficult one for many philosophers to cross, and it certainly slowed receptivity.

Sartreanism also evolved from a philosophy that most Americans, because of their lack of proficiency in French, could directly access in only one slim capsulization—*Existentialism*—to a body of thought in which nine major philosophical works were available. The translation process was almost complete by the last phase of early Sartreanism's introduction. Between 1957 and 1963 interest spread to the point that scholars were now reaching back to Sartre's first studies to understand the roots; works written in the 1930s were translated to satisfy that curiosity. Also reflective of the progression from an almost untranslated body of thought to one in which important English versions existed was the decrease in the time that it took for some of these translations to emerge.

The American sojourn of early Sartreanism was long enough to advance through what William James labeled "the classic stages of a theory's career."[64] Novel ideas initially met with a great deal of hostile resistance, said James, but slowly individuals acknowledged some merit in the new concepts. Finally, clear parallels with ideas and methods already embraced slowly came into better focus and people began to believe that they had independently discovered Sartre's concepts. The growing identification of Sartreanism with James's strain of pragmatism illustrated such a progression.

But Sartreanism was never thoroughly Americanized in the postwar years. Although some philosophers readily acknowledged links between Sartre's constructs and James's radical empiricism, few went beyond the dissection of the French philosophy and the affirmation of discrete ideas that complemented existing perspectives. Why was Sartreanism unassimilable in its entirety? The influence of the analytic perspective was significant, but that tradition was clearly not the only root of the reluctance to adopt the French philosophy. While the analytic viewpoint was a powerful one, many of the leading voices in American philosophy roundly criticized analytic methodology for its lack of breadth. In fact, existentialism sometimes became ammunition against the influence of narrowly conceived analytic thought; philosophers commended it as one philosophy that did not neglect human experience.

The chief philosophical disagreements Americans had with Sartreanism concerned subjectivity, intersubjectivity, and objectivity. As mentioned above, subjectively determined truths and values were viewed very skeptically by most philosophers. The activity of intersubjective thinking was a necessary step along the path toward knowledge and ethical action; knowledge was not privately obtained but rather acquired through a process of public inquiry.[65]

Philosophers also characterized early Sartreanism as a strain of thought that belittled faith in reason, and this negative perspective prodded many to reject it. Even though informed observers pointed out the strong overtones of Cartesian rationalism in Sartre's ideas, they often did not succeed in offsetting the common view that Sartre made irrationalism too prominent a factor in human thought. While a growing minority of philosophers steered toward an emotional acceptance of reason's dethronement—given the evidence of world wars and political atrocities—most were unwilling to whittle away at the explanatory power of rational thought within their discipline. They readily acknowledged, however, that Sartreanism expressed an emotional mood that reflected an erosion of confidence in rationality.[66]

An optimistic outlook toward the future was connected to this enduring belief in the wisdom of the philosophical application of reason. Rational thought and sanguinity were joined features in the liberal ideology that permeated American philosophy. But just as there were cracks in reason, there were ruptures in optimism. The key ingredients of liberalism were besieged at midcentury. For most American philosophers, optimism won out; Sartreanism seemed simply too pessimistic. No matter how much sensitive scholars like Barnes tried to highlight optimistic notes by creating book titles such as *The Literature of Possibility* to remind people that the individual, existence, and the future were potentialities in Sartre's scheme, they were not very successful in the end. When Kurtz reflected upon the general discontent with Sartre's dour tone in his 1961 overview "Kierkegaard, Existentialism, and the Contemporary Scene," he concluded that the optimistic tenor of American thought might be a product of naïveté, but ultimately cheerfulness was superior to despair. Pessimism, Kurtz observed commonsensically, would not motivate people; it did not "provide the challenging impetus for a good life."[67]

Sartreanism also suffered because of its hostility to religion. For some who considered religion simply a dead letter, Sartre's dramatically formulated atheism posed no difficulty. For many others, however, it was an affront to religious beliefs. Plantinga at Wayne State University later recalled that many of his colleagues had at least a "grass roots interest in theology."[68] They may not have been overtly religious, observed Plantinga, but they were not far removed from the spiritual traditions of their families and communities, and they were averse to a philosophy that trampled too indelicately on remaining religious sensibilities.

Sartreanism's rejection of philosophical specialization was another source of its inability to enter the philosophical mainstream. The whole ethos of midcentury American philosophy was permeated by the importance of specializing—of circumscribing one's inquiries in order to present more finely detailed analyses. Of course this did not mean that all philosophers produced only narrowly conceived systems, but only that the virtues of specialization were readily acknowledged by many in the community. One of Barrett's chief complaints in *Irrational Man* was that philosophers sometimes did not see that restricted vision could be a problematic side effect of specialization.[69]

Sartreanism itself was touched by the specializing bent in America; key concepts were examined separately rather than within the context of the totality of Sartre's thought. When the aesthetician Ames, for example, took a first look at Sartre's concept of human existence in 1950, he labeled it irrational because he would not consider the validity of the formulation within Sartre's phenomenological ontology. One reason for Barnes's willingness to take on the massive task of translating *Being and Nothingness* was her desire to counteract this inclination to separate the threads of Sartreanism without troubling to reunite them.

Finally, the philosophy suffered from its political connections. Neither its interpretation as a form of misbegotten liberalism nor as an experiment in adaptive Marxism won much favor in America. Philosophers like Kurtz at Union College who read it as an expression of the erosion of the liberal faith in reason fretted that such a doctrine would be politically dangerous to the noncommunist West; at the same time, philosophers like Sidney Hook feared Sartreanism's attempt to become compatible with Marxism.

Although Sartreanism was not institutionalized in American philosophy as the "American existentialism" that Rice argued for so passionately in 1956, it did find spots of entry because of particular qualities that meshed well with existing characteristics. Although powerful currents like analytic philosophy created important obstacles, the American philosophical scene was open to the introduction if not the total acceptance of new ideas. The community was not one in which one point of view or method had an unyielding stranglehold; a distinctive ingredient was a certain degree of fluidity and receptivity to new ideas.[70] Throughout its history, American philosophy was enriched by the entrance of European thought; Sartreanism was at least not confronted by an absolutely impenetrable barrier to nonindigenous systems.

A thematic current that facilitated existentialism's American reception was the value it attached to ethical issues. Although many American philosophers at midcentury were enamored of various strains of analytic thought, some felt guilty when their work narrowed to the point where moral questions were completely forgotten. That ethical concern was alive and well during these years was very clear from the American Philosophical Association's presidential addresses. Repeatedly, presidents made clear their belief that their role as watchdogs of the profession included making colleagues feel culpable when they ignored contemporary ethical problems. Paul A. Schilpp, at Northwestern, for example, titled his address to the Western Division in 1959 "The Abdication of Philosophy." As one of the respected senior statesmen of the profession, he browbeat his colleagues for deserting "true philosophy" for linguistic analysis: "We will be linguists, semanticists, symbolists, grammarians—yes, even logicians. But we will not be philosophers."[71] Schilpp's essential plea was for the primacy of ethical issues in contemporary life.

The centrality of experience in American philosophical discourse— the reigning belief that conceptual frameworks should be grounded in everyday existence—connected positively with Sartreanism too. The elemental weight of experience was clearly visible in the use Sartre made of phenomenology. This emphasis on knowledge gained through observation bonded easily with many American philosophers' predilections. John Randall, leader of the naturalistic school at Columbia, made the point very well when he warned others to be wary of approaching philosophy through the analysis of words rather than through the empirical observation of existence. In his address to the Eastern Division of the American Philosophical Association in 1956, Randall exhorted his colleagues to follow the example of Gyges in Herodotus's *History*. When Gyges heard about the marvelous beauty of the king's wife, Randall explained, he decided to see for himself rather than rely on hearsay. With tongue in cheek, Randall held up Gyges to his audience as "no timid Oxford don, but a real philosopher—almost an American." Employing the rich and colloquial philosophical language of William James to evoke favorable sensibilities in his audience, Randall heaped praise on Gyges's experiential approach. "Now for my money," he said, "that is a tough-minded, genuinely American philosophy."[72]

Sartrean individualism also touched a powerful American ideological theme and a major nerve. Sartre urged the discipline to make the individual a wellspring of meaning and value, and Americans listened carefully to this message. Philosophers universally applauded Sartre's desire to reinfuse the profession with a sense of the merit of the subjective perspective, but the great majority quickly rejected any subjectivity unconstrained by the boundaries of logical thought or community-determined values.

What positive impact did Sartreanism have on a philosophical environment that already blended dominant themes of relative openness, ethical concerns, the centrality of experience, and an appreciation of the individual as a legitimate philosophical focus? Above all, Sartreanism served as a prod that helped revitalize these themes at a point in American philosophy when they seemed to be losing ground. Many mourned the dethroning of philosophy as the source of wisdom in the first half of the twentieth century; science, it sometimes seemed, had taken philosophy's place. Sartreanism helped reinvigorate the discipline by infusing it with a line of inquiry that led back to questions of immediate human importance. And because of its links with other fields of study, Sartreanism injected an energizing interdisciplinary perspective.

Sartreanism also helped propel the philosophical pendulum away from the threatened but never achieved hegemony of analysis. Opposition to logical positivism and linguistic analysis had existed from the beginning of their American influence in the 1930s, and by midcentury some metaphysically minded and socially active philosophers encouraged rejection of the analytic program and viewpoint. For a few philosophers, Sartreanism provided another arena in which to explore issues outside the analytic model.

The French philosophy also highlighted the need for dialogue between those who approached philosophy from radically different perspectives. Commentators continually lamented the frequent inability of analytic and speculative philosophers to communicate with one another in discussions of Sartreanism's vices and virtues. Philosophers of other persuasions felt the prod too. Even Hook, one of the most fervent opponents of Sartreanism, invited existentialists to help build a framework that could be shared by philosophers of many schools.[73] In the same vein, Sartreanism's emergence in the United States reminded philosophers of the need for international exchange in their discipline. The difficulty of understanding Sartre's concepts when translations were limited and the slowness of recognizing that the school was rooted in established Continental traditions highlighted the wisdom of increasing international communication. The beckoning hope that better philosophical conversations between countries at opposite ends of the ideological spectrum would promote world peace was a larger cultural factor underlying this desire for internationalism.

Sartre's concepts resonated especially loudly in the ears of younger philosophers and their students. Just as Sartreanism first found most of its adherents among students in Paris, so it had greater appeal for younger Americans. One reason for this was Sartreanism's novelty and its strident rejection of traditional philosophy. Although older people certainly could be attracted to new schools of thought, there was an even greater affinity between youth and whatever was current. A commonsensical explanation existed for this tendency. Older philosophers, having already consolidated their identities and careers around other beliefs, had a vested interest in maintaining established perspectives; trained in other intellectual traditions, they made choices and solidified careers in which those decisions played a critical role. Younger scholars and students tended to be more receptive to new philosophies as their careers and personal identities were often not yet so attached to a particular philosophical perspective. More important, the substantive question that Sartreanism asked was a definitive one for people in early adulthood: "What is the meaning of individual existence?"

Some women philosophers too were attracted to Sartreanism because it provided them with an opportunity to enter a male-dominated profession. Because there were so few American philosophers trained in Continental existentialism, departments were more willing to employ women to teach courses on existentialism, and publishers more likely to have women translate or critique the philosophy.

In the final analysis, Sartreanism's most significant impact on the American philosophical community was to force some individuals to question the legitimacy of their philosophical premises. Even philosophers like Kurtz who found so much to worry over in Sartreanism noted approvingly that "existentialism . . . has compelled us to radically examine once again our basic presuppositions, for it has brought to light new facts and values that we overlooked."[74] Both the positive reading of Sartreanism as a philosophy that prompted a greater appreciation of the significance of freedom, and the negative interpretation of Sartreanism as a school that overemphasized the irrationality of human consciousness, encouraged the scrutiny of fundamental premises. It was the coexistence of these opposing readings that gave Sartreanism its great dynamism within American philosophy and made it for many Americans such an arresting analysis of the human condition.

CHAPTER ONE

1. Throughout, works will be cited by their French titles when their original publication and their French impact are discussed and by English titles when their publication in English and their American impact are discussed. See Jean-Paul Sartre, *Search for a Method,* trans. Hazel Barnes (New York: Knopf, 1963).

2. David Newhall, interviewed by the author, Portland, 20 May 1979.

3. Jean-Paul Sartre, *Being and Nothingness: A Phenomenological Essay on Ontology,* trans. Hazel Barnes (New York: Washington Square, 1956), and *Existentialism,* trans. Bernard Frechtman (New York: Philosophical Library, 1947).

4. James Collins, *The Existentialists: A Critical Study* (Chicago: Henry Regnery, 1952), 188–217; William Barrett, *Irrational Man: A Study in Existential Philosophy* (Garden City, N.J.: Doubleday, 1958), 3–36; Marjorie Grene, *Dreadful Freedom: A Critique of Existentialism* (Chicago: University of Chicago Press, 1948), 1–14; Ronald Grimsley, *Existentialist Thought* (Cardiff: University of Wales Press, 1967), 212–17; Robert Olson, *An Introduction to Existentialism* (New York: Dover, 1962), 1–134.

5. Collins, *The Existentialists,* 5–17; Grene, *Dreadful Freedom,* 122–41; Grimsley, *Existentialist Thought,* 12–39; George Rupp, *Beyond Existentialism and Zen: Religion in a Pluralistic World* (London: Oxford University Press, 1979), 39–47.

6. Collins, *The Existentialists,* 3–26; Grene, *Dreadful Freedom,* 15–41; Thomas Flynn, *Sartre and Marxist Existentialism: The Test Case of Collective Responsibility* (Chicago: University of Chicago Press, 1984), 173–78.

7. Barrett, *Irrational Man,* 149–76; Dominick La Capra, *A Preface to Sartre* (Ithaca, N.Y.: Cornell University Press, 1978), 152–53; Thomas Hanna, *The Lyrical Existentialists* (New York: Atheneum, 1962), 15–105; Alastair Hannay, *Kierkegaard* (London: Routledge and Kegan, 1982), 1–19.

8. Collins, *The Existentialists,* 17–25; Hanna, *The Lyrical Existentialists,* 105–87; Frederick Copleston, *Friedrich Nietzsche: Philosopher of Culture* (London: Search Press, 1975), 29–116.

9. Flynn, *Sartre and Marxist Existentialism,* 173–78.

10. Jean-Paul Sartre, *The Words,* trans. Bernard Frechtman (New York: Braziller, 1964), 18.

11. Ronald Hayman, *Sartre: A Life* (New York: Simon and Schuster, 1987), 35.

12. Paul Schilpp, ed., *The Philosophy of Jean-Paul Sartre* (La Salle, Ill.: Open Court, 1981), 6.

13. Simone de Beauvoir, *The Prime of Life,* trans. Peter Green (New York: Harper, 1962), 18.

14. Hayman, *Sartre,* 100.

15. Jean-Paul Sartre, *Imagination: A Psychological Critique,* trans. Forrest Williams (Ann Arbor: University of Michigan Press, 1962), and *Nausea,* trans. Lloyd Alexander (Norfolk, Conn.: New Directions, n.d.).

16. Jean-Paul Sartre, *The Transcendence of the Ego: An Existentialist Theory of Con-

sciousness, trans. Forrest Williams and Robert Kirkpatrick (New York: Noonday, 1957).

17. Jean-Paul Sartre, *The Psychology of the Imagination,* trans. Bernard Frechtman (New York: Philosophical Library, 1948), and *The Emotions: Outline of a Theory,* trans. Bernard Frechtman (New York: Philosophical Library, 1948).

18. Alain Ranwez, *Jean-Paul Sartre's Les Temps Modernes: A Literary History, 1945–1962* (Troy, N.Y.: Whitson, 1981), 32–58.

19. Karl Marx, *Early Writings,* ed. and trans. T. B. Bottomore (New York: McGraw-Hill, 1964).

20. Hayman, *Sartre,* 325.

21. Annie Cohen-Solal, *Sartre: A Life,* trans. Anna Cancogni (New York: Pantheon, 1987), 404.

22. Jean-Paul Sartre, *Critique of Dialectical Reason: Theory of Practical Ensembles,* trans. A. Sheridan-Smith (London: Humanities, 1976), and *Search for a Method.*

23. Beauvoir, *The Prime of Life,* 18.

24. Jean-Paul Sartre, *The War Diaries,* trans. Quintin Hoare (New York: Pantheon, 1985), 86.

25. Wilfrid Desan, *The Marxism of Jean-Paul Sartre* (New York: Doubleday, 1966), 260–61.

26. Collins, *The Existentialists,* 50.

27. La Capra, *A Preface to Sartre,* 129.

28. Collins, *The Existentialists,* 57–58.

29. Mark Poster, *Existential Marxism in Postwar France: From Sartre to Althusser* (Princeton, N.J.: Princeton University Press, 1975), 20.

30. Janet Flanner, *Paris Journal,* vol. 1, *1944–1965* (New York: Atheneum, 1965), 49.

31. Hayman, *Sartre,* 206.

32. Simone de Beauvoir, *Force of Circumstance,* trans. Richard Howard (New York: Putnam, 1963).

33. H. Stuart Hughes, *The Obstructed Path: French Social Thought in the Years of Desperation, 1930–1960* (New York: Harper, 1968), 163.

34. Edith Kern, ed., *Sartre: A Collection of Essays* (Englewood Cliffs, N.J.: Prentice-Hall, 1962), 17.

35. Wade Baskin, ed., *Essays in Existentialism* (New York: Citadel, 1965), 3.

36. Hayman, *Sartre,* 217.

37. Flanner, *Paris Journal,* 10.

38. Hayman, *Sartre,* 20.

39. Dorothy Pickles, *France between the Republics* (London: Love and Malcolmson, 1946), 151.

40. Ranwez, *Jean-Paul Sartre's Les Temps Modernes,* 40.

41. Jacques Havet, "French Philosophical Traditions between the Two Wars," in *Philosophic Thought in France and the United States: Essays Representing Major Trends in French and American Philosophy,* ed. Marvin Farber (Albany: State University of New York Press, 1950), 30.

42. Sartre, *Search for a Method,* 19.

43. Herbert Spiegelberg, *The Phenomenological Movement: A Historical Introduction,* vol. 2 (The Hague: Nijhoff, 1960), 410–12.

44. Poster, *Existential Marxism in Postwar France,* 18.

45. Ibid., 58–63.

46. Richard McKeon, "An American Reaction to the Present Situation in French Philosophy," in Farber, ed., 360; see also Jean Wahl, "The Present Situation and the Present Future of French Philosophy," in Farber, ed., 38.

47. McKeon, "An American Reaction," 360.

48. Vincent Descombes, *Modern French Philosophy,* trans. L. Scott-Fox and J. M. Harding (London: Cambridge University Press, 1980), 7.

CHAPTER TWO

1. William Barrett, *What Is Existentialism?* (1947; reprint, New York: Grove, 1964), 22 (page citations are to the reprint edition).

2. This conclusion is based on my personal correspondence with twenty American philosophers. When asked if they attended Sartre's plays and lectures between 1945 and 1947, all responded negatively.

3. Robert Cumming, letter to author, 23 October 1979; Stuart Brown, Jr., letter to author, 21 June 1990.

4. Robert Cohn, letter to author, 19 October 1979.

5. Arthur Danto, letter to author, 30 December 1989.

6. Jean-Paul Sartre, *No Exit (Huis Clos): A Play in One Act and The Flies (Les Mouches): A Play in Three Acts,* trans. Stuart Gilbert (New York: Knopf, 1947), *The Age of Reason,* trans. Eric Sutton (New York: Knopf, 1947), and *The Reprieve,* trans. Eric Sutton (New York: Knopf, 1947).

7. Robert Cohn, letter to author, 19 October 1979.

8. Henri Peyre, letter to author, 10 August 1979.

9. Ibid.; Judith Schiff, letter to author, 21 November 1988.

10. Henri Peyre, *French Novelists of Today* (New York: Oxford University Press, 1967), 244–74.

11. Jean Wahl, "Existentialism: A Preface," *New Republic,* October 1945, 442.

12. Annie Cohen-Solal, *Sartre: A Life,* trans. Anna Cancogni (New York: Pantheon, 1987), 275.

13. Otto Kraushaar, review of *A Kierkegaard Anthology,* edited by Robert Bretall, *Existentialism* by Jean-Paul Sartre, and "What Is Existentialism?" by William Barrett, *Journal of Philosophy* 44 (December 1947): 715.

14. David Newhall, telephone conversation with author, 31 October 1990; Forrest Williams, telephone conversation with author, 30 July 1990.

15. Jean-Paul Sartre, *Existentialism,* trans. Bernard Frechtman (New York: Philosophical Library, 1947), 18.

16. Selections from *L'Être et le néant* appeared in Jean-Paul Sartre, *Existential Psychoanalysis,* trans. Hazel Barnes (Chicago: Henry Regnery, 1953).

17. Robert Cornish, letter to author, 13 October 1989.

18. Robert Cornish, letter to author, 27 March 1989.

19. Joseph Fell, letter to author, 31 March 1980.

20. Cohen-Solal, *Sartre,* 271.

21. "Existentialism," *Time,* 28 January 1946, 28.

22. Jacques Barzun, "Ça Existe: A Note on the New Ism," *American Scholar,* October 1946, 449.

23. Albert Guerard, "French and American Pessimism," *Harper's Magazine,* September 1945, 276; Bernard Frizell, "Existentialism: Postwar Paris Enthrones a Bleak Philosophy of Pessimism," *Life,* 7 June 1946, 59; Oliver Barres, "In the Deeps of Despair," *Saturday Review of Literature,* 31 May 1947, 14.

24. Barres, "In the Deeps of Despair," 14; John Lackey Brown, "Paris, 1946: Its Three War Philosophies," *New York Times,* 1 September 1946.

25. J. Alvarez del Vayo, "Politics and the Intellectual," *Nation,* 28 September 1946, 349.

26. Frizell, "Existentialism," 59.

27. John Lackey Brown, "Chief Prophet of Existentialism," *New York Times Magazine,* 2 February 1947, 20.

28. Ibid.

29. Frizell, "Existentialism," 59.

30. "Pursuit of Wisdom: Existentialism, Lettrism and Sensorialism," *Time,* 2 December 1946, 20; Frizell, "Existentialism," 59.

31. Simone de Beauvoir, *Force of Circumstance,* trans. Richard Howard (New York: Putnam, 1964), 33.

32. John Lackey Brown, "De Gaulle Foes Paid by U.S., Paris Is Told," *New York Times,* 25 January 1945.

33. Letter to the Editor, *New York Times,* 1 February 1945.

34. Jean-Paul Sartre, "Americans and Their Myths," *Nation,* 18 October 1947, 403.

35. Brown, "Chief Prophet of Existentialism," 21; "Pursuit of Wisdom," 31.

36. Frizell, "Existentialism," 59; Brown, "Chief Prophet of Existentialism," 21.

37. Barres, "In the Deeps of Despair," 14.

38. Justus Buchler, "Concerning *Existentialism,*" *Nation* 25 October 1947, 449.

39. William Barrett, *Irrational Man: A Study in Existential Philosophy* (Garden City, N.Y.: Doubleday, 1958), 10.

40. Bruce Kuklick, *The Rise of American Philosophy: Cambridge, Massachusetts, 1860–1930* (New Haven, Conn.: Yale University Press, 1977), xxi.

41. Brand Blanshard, "From the Commissioner's Mailbag," *Philosophical Review* 54 (May 1945): 210–16.

42. Barrett, *What Is Existentialism?* 22–28.

43. Ibid., 20.

44. Simone de Beauvoir, "Strictly Personal: Jean-Paul Sartre," trans. Malcolm Cowley, *Harper's Bazaar,* January 1946, 113.

45. Buchler, "Concerning Existentialism," 449; Marjorie Grene, "L'Homme est une passion inutile: Sartre et Heidegger," *Kenyon Review* 9 (Spring 1947): 177; William Barrett, "The Talent and Career of Jean-Paul Sartre," *Partisan Review,* Spring 1946, 239.

46. Sartre, *Being and Nothingness: A Phenomenological Essay on Ontology,* trans. Hazel Barnes (New York: Washington Square, 1956), 615.

47. Kraushaar, review, 717; Buchler, "Concerning Existentialism," 449; Barrett, *What Is Existentialism?* 83.

48. Joseph Blau, *Men and Movements in American Philosophy* (New York: Prentice-Hall, 1952), 314–22; Andrew Reck, *Recent American Philosophy: Studies of Ten Representative Thinkers* (New York: Pantheon, 1964), xx.

49. Buchler, "Concerning Existentialism," 449.

50. Edwin Burtt, "What Happened in Philosophy from 1900 to 1950," *Allegheny College Bulletin* 7 (May 1952): 16.

51. Barrett, *What Is Existentialism?* 27.

52. Roy Sellars, review of *Existentialism,* by Jean-Paul Sartre, *American Sociological Review* 12 (October 1947): 725.

53. Grene, "L'Homme est une passion inutile," 184.

54. Sartre, *Existentialism,* 29.

55. Grene, "L'Homme est une passion inutile," 177.

56. Iris Murdoch, *Sartre: Romantic Rationalist* (London: Bowes and Bowes, 1953), 105–13.

57. Kraushaar, review, 721.

58. Ibid.

59. Ibid., 717.

60. Buchler, "Concerning Existentialism," 449.

61. Barrett, *What Is Existentialism?* 9, and "Talent and Career of Jean-Paul Sartre," 244.

62. Barrett, *What Is Existentialism?* 109.

63. Kraushaar, review, 120, 717, 720, 721.

64. Buchler, "Concerning Existentialism," 449; Sellars, 726.

65. Sellars, review, 725.

66. David Riesman, with Nathan Glazer and Reuel Denny, *The Lonely Crowd: A Study of the Changing American Character* (New Haven, Conn.: Yale University Press, 1950); William Whyte, *The Organization Man* (New York: Simon and Schuster, 1956).

67. Catherine Rau, telephone conversation with author, 21 April 1989.

CHAPTER THREE

1. Jean-Paul Sartre, *The Emotions: Outline of a Theory,* trans. Bernard Frechtman (New York: Philosophical Library, 1948), and *The Psychology of the Imagination,* trans. Bernard Frechtman (New York: Philosophical Library, 1948).

2. Sidney Hook, review of *The Emotions,* by Jean-Paul Sartre, *New York Times,* 11 July 1948, 16.

3. Maurice Natanson, *A Critique of Jean-Paul Sartre's Ontology* (Lincoln: University of Nebraska Press, 1951).

4. Catherine Rau, telephone conversation with author, 21 April 1989.

5. Arthur Danto, letter to author, 30 December 1989.

6. Ibid.

7. Eugene Kaelin, letter to author, 24 October 1987.

8. Eugene Kaelin, letter to author, 9 July 1989.

9. Marvin Farber, ed., *Philosophic Thought in France and the United States: Essays Representing Major Trends in French and American Philosophy* (Albany: State University of New York Press, 1950).

10. Martin Heidegger, *Existence and Being,* trans. Douglass Scott, R. F. C. Hull, and Alan Crick (Chicago: Henry Regnery, 1949).

11. Sartre, *The Emotions,* 12–30.

12. Marjorie Grene, "Sartre's Theory of the Emotions," *Yale French Studies* 1 (Spring–Summer 1948): 97–101.

13. Ibid., 101.

14. Jean-Paul Sartre, *What Is Literature?* trans. Bernard Frechtman (New York: Philosophical Library, 1949), and *The Psychology of the Imagination.*

15. Thomas Munro, "Present Tendencies in American Aesthetics," in Farber, ed., 655–69.

16. Ibid., 658.

17. Sartre, *The Psychology of the Imagination,* 14–18.

18. Hook, review, 16.

19. Ibid.

20. Van Meter Ames, "Existentialism and the Arts," *Journal of Aesthetics and Art Criticism* 8 (March 1951): 254–55, 256; Catherine Rau, "The Aesthetic Views of Jean-Paul Sartre," *Journal of Aesthetics and Art Criticism* 9 (Winter 1950): 146–47.

21. Rau, "The Aesthetic Views of Jean-Paul Sartre," 147; Ames, "Existentialism and the Arts," 256.

22. William Barrett, "The End of Modern Literature: Existentialism and Crisis," in Literary Opinion in America, ed. Morton Zabel (New York: Harper, 1951), 751.

23. Roy Sellars, review of *Existentialism,* by Jean-Paul Sartre, *American Sociological Review* 12 (October 1947): 726; Catherine Rau, "The Ethical Theory of Jean-Paul Sartre," *Journal of Philosophy* 46 (August 1949): 545.

24. Marjorie Grene, *Dreadful Freedom: A Critique of Existentialism* (Chicago: University of Chicago Press, 1948), 8–10.

25. Richard McKeon, "An American Reaction to the Present Situation in French Philosophy," 337.

26. Ibid., 360.

27. John Smith, "Is Existence a Valid Philosophical Concept?" *Journal of Philosophy* 47 (April 1950): 238–49.

28. Ibid., 246.

29. Ibid., 247.

30. Philip Rice, "The Children of Narcissus: Some Themes of French Speculation," *Kenyon Review* 12 (Winter 1950): 117–37.

31. Mary Coolidge, "Some Vicissitudes of the Once-Born and of the Twice-Born Man," *Philosophy and Phenomenological Research* 11 (September 1950): 75–87.

32. Ibid., 75.

33. Ibid., 84–85.

34. Ibid., 87.

35. Hazel Barnes, "Existentialism in America" (lecture presented at the University of Colorado, Boulder, 28 July 1960).

36. Maurice Natanson, telephone conversation with author, 1 April 1989.

37. Otto Kraushaar, review of *A Kierkegaard Anthology,* edited by Robert Bretall, *Existentialism* by Jean-Paul Sartre, and "What Is Existentialism?" by William Barrett, *Journal of Philosophy* 44 (December 1947): 717.

38. Grene, *Dreadful Freedom,* 98.

39. John Smith, letter to author, 6 March 1989.

40. Herbert Marcuse, "Remarks on Jean-Paul Sartre's *L'Être et le néant,*" *Philosophy and Phenomenological Research* 8 (March 1948): 311.

41. Grene, *Dreadful Freedom,* 98; Catherine Rau, telephone conversation with author, 21 April 1989.

42. Marjorie Grene, *Philosophy In and Out of Europe* (Berkeley: University of California Press, 1976), ix.

43. Stuart Brown, "The Atheistic Existentialism of Jean-Paul Sartre," *Philosophical Review* 57 (March 1948): 158–66.

44. Stuart Brown, letter to author, 21 June 1990.

45. Stuart Brown, "The Atheistic Existentialism of Jean-Paul Sartre," 166.

46. Sidney Hook, *Out of Step: An Unquiet Life in the Twentieth Century* (New York: Harper, 1987), 399.

47. Ibid., 400.

48. Barrett, "The End of Modern Literature," 751.

49. V. M. Ames, "Fetishism in the Existentialism of Sartre," *Journal of Philosophy* 47 (July 1950): 407–11.

50. Grace de Laguna, "Speculative Philosophy," *Philosophical Review* 60 (January 1950): 3–19.

51. Natanson, *A Critique of Jean-Paul Sartre's Ontology,* 113.

52. Marcuse, "Remarks on Jean-Paul Sartre's *L'Être et le néant,*" 309–10.

53. Ames, "Fetishism in the Existentialism of Sartre," 407.

54. Ibid., 409, 410.

55. Maurice Natanson, "Sartre's Fetishism: A Reply to Van Meter Ames," *Journal of Philosophy* 48 (February 1951): 95–99.

56. Ibid., 98, 99.

57. V. M. Ames, "Reply to Mr. Natanson," *Journal of Philosophy* 48 (February 1951): 99, 101, 102.

58. John Yolton, "The Metaphysic of *En-soi* and *Pour-soi,*" *Journal of Philosophy* 48 (February 1951), 556.

59. Ibid., 549.

60. Rice, "The Children of Narcissus," 119.

61. Francis Randall, letter to author, 24 November 1979.

62. Jean-Paul Sartre, *Being and Nothingness: A Phenomenological Essay on Ontology,* trans. Hazel Barnes (New York: Washington Square, 1956), 86–116.

63. Grene, *Dreadful Freedom,* 10.

64. Brown, "The Atheistic Existentialism of Jean-Paul Sartre," 166.

65. J. Glenn Gray, "The Idea of Death in Existentialism," *Journal of Philosophy* 48 (March 1951): 124–26.

66. Grene, *Philosophy In and Out of Europe,* 50.

67. Gray, "The Idea of Death in Existentialism," 124, 125.

68. V. J. McGill, "Sartre's Doctrine of Freedom," *Revue Internationale de Philosophie* 9 (July 1949): 329.

69. *University of Chicago Catalogue* (Chicago: University of Chicago Press, 1948), 25; *Columbia University Catalogue* (New York: Columbia University Press, 1948), 105.

70. Hazel Barnes, letter to author, 11 June 1979.

71. *Harvard University Catalogue* (Cambridge, Mass.: Harvard University Press, 1950), 209; Willard Quine, letter to author, 10 September 1979.

72. Joan Duffy, letter to author, 7 September 1988.

73. Joseph Fell, letter to author, 31 March 1980.

74. Ibid.

75. Hazel Barnes, letter to author, 11 June 1979; Maxine Greene, letter to author, 11 June 1979.

76. Maurice Natanson, telephone conversation with author, 1 April 1989.

77. Marjorie Grene, "In and Out of Friendship," in *Human Nature and Natural Knowledge,* ed. A. Donagan, A. N. Perovich, Jr., and M. V. Weden (Dordrecht: D. Reidel, 1986), 360.

78. Ibid.

79. Ibid., 361; Marjorie Grene, letter to author, 6 December 1988.

80. Catherine Rau, telephone conversation with author, 21 April 1989; Hazel Barnes, telephone conversation with author, 1 May 1979.

81. William Wright, "The End of the Day," *Philosophical Review* 55 (1946): 326.

CHAPTER FOUR

1. Philip Rice, "Existentialism and the Self," *Kenyon Review* 12 (Spring 1950): 304; Jean-Paul Sartre, *Being and Nothingness: A Phenomenological Essay on Ontology,* trans. Hazel Barnes (New York: Washington Square, 1956), ix.

2. Jean-Paul Sartre, *Existential Psychoanalysis,* trans. Hazel Barnes (Chicago: Henry Regnery, 1953); Walter Kaufmann, *Existentialism from Dostoevsky to Sartre* (New York: Meridian, 1956).

3. Kaufmann, *Existentialism,* 45–48.

4. Elisabeth Young-Bruehl, *Freedom and Karl Jaspers's Philosophy* (New Haven, Conn.: Yale University Press, 1981), 59–81.

5. Ludwig Binswanger, *Being-in-the-World: Selected Papers of Ludwig Binswanger,* trans. Jacob Needleman (New York: Basic, 1963), 48; Raymond Corsini, ed., *Current Psychotherapies* (Itasca, Ill.: F. E. Peacock, 1973), 319.

6. Sartre, *Being and Nothingness,* 712–33.

7. Alfred Stern, *Sartre: His Philosophy and Existential Psychoanalysis* (New York: Delacorte, 1953).

8. Ibid., 190–212.

9. Wilfrid Desan, *The Tragic Finale: An Essay on the Philosophy of Jean-Paul Sartre* (Cambridge, Mass.: Harvard University Press, 1954).

10. Wilfrid Desan, letter to author, 29 June 1990.

11. American Philosophical Association, *Proceedings of the Fifty-First Annual Meeting of the Western Division* (Yellow Springs, Ohio: American Philosophical Association, 1956), 30.

12. Mark Poster, *Existential Marxism in Postwar France: From Sartre to Althusser* (Princeton, N.J.: Princeton University Press, 1975), 164.

13. Ibid., 183–85.

14. Ronald Hayman, *Sartre: A Life* (New York: Simon and Schuster, 1987), 282–83.

15. Albert Camus, *L'Homme révolté* (Paris: Gallimard, 1952).

16. Hayman, *Sartre: A Life*, 282–83.

17. Nicola Chiarmonte, "Paris Letter: Sartre v. Camus, A Political Quarrel," *Partisan Review* 19 (November–December 1952): 680; Brand Blanshard, letter to author, 11 November 1979; Maurice Natanson, letter to author, 4 July 1990; Kaufmann, *Existentialism*, 48.

18. Sidney Hook, "Symposium: Our Country and Our Culture," *Partisan Review* 19 (July–August 1952): 572.

19. Herbert Spiegelberg, "French Existentialism: Its Social Philosophies," *Kenyon Review* 16 (Summer 1954): 448.

20. Ibid.

21. American Philosophical Association, *Proceedings of the Fifty-First Annual Meeting of the Western Division* 40.

22. Maurice Natanson, "Jean-Paul Sartre's Philosophy of Freedom," *Social Research* 19 (September 1952): 364–80; Morton White, *The Age of Analysis: Twentieth Century Philosophers*, vol. 6, *The Great Ages of Western Philosophy* (Boston: Houghton-Mifflin, 1955): 116; Stern, *Sartre*, 25.

23. Kaufmann, *Existentialism*, 45.

24. Stern, *Sartre*, 250; Albert Levi, "The Quixotic Quest for Being," *Ethics* 66 (January 1956): 132.

25. Joseph Fell, letter to author, 31 March 1980.

26. Charles Hendel, "The Subjective as a Problem," *Philosophical Review* 62 (July 1953): 327–54.

27. John Wild, *The Challenge of Existentialism* (Bloomington: Indiana University Press, 1953), 9.

28. Hendel, "The Subjective as a Problem," 339–40; Wild, *The Challenge of Existentialism*, 7.

29. Hendel, "The Subjective as a Problem," 352.

30. Ibid., 339.

31. Ibid., 341.

32. Wild, *The Challenge of Existentialism*, 243–46.

33. White, *The Age of Analysis*, 238; George Schrader, "Existence, Truth and Subjectivity," *Journal of Philosophy* 53 (November 1956): 759–71.

34. White, *The Age of Analysis*, 238; Schrader, "Existence, Truth and Subjectivity," 762.

35. Sartre, *Being and Nothingness,* xliii.

36. Ibid., 119–59.

37. Desan, *The Tragic Finale,* 149–59.

38. Thomas Anderson, *The Foundation and Structure of Sartrean Ethics* (Lawrence, Kans.: Regents, 1979), 68.

39. William Earle, "Freedom and Existence: A Symposium," *Review of Metaphysics* 9 (September 1955): 46.

40. Desan, *The Tragic Finale,* 140–56.

41. Ibid., 162; Robert Olson, *An Introduction to Existentialism* (New York: Dover, 1962), 179.

42. Earle, "Freedom and Existence," 47–49.

43. Ibid., 54, 55.

44. Desan, *The Tragic Finale,* 185.

45. Sidney Hook, "The Quest for 'Being,'" *Journal of Philosophy* 50 (November 1953): 709–31; John Randall, "Metaphysics: Its Function, Consequences, and Criteria," *Journal of Philosophy* 63 (July 1946): 401–12.

46. Hook, "The Quest for 'Being,'" 716–25.

47. John Randall, "On Being Rejected," *Journal of Philosophy* 50 (December 1953): 797–805.

48. Ibid., 798.

49. Hendel, "The Subjective as a Problem," 350.

50. John Smith, "The Revolt of Existence," *Yale Review* 43 (March 1954): 364–71.

51. Ibid., 370–71.

52. Hazel Barnes, interview by author, tape recording, Boulder, Colo., 1979.

53. Sartre, *Being and Nothingness,* iii.

54. William James, *The Varieties of Religious Experience: A Study in Human Nature* (New York: Modern Library, 1936).

55. Barnes, interview by author, tape recording, Boulder, Colo., 1979.

56. Sartre, *Being and Nothingness,* xxxiv.

57. Ibid., x.

58. William Barrett, "Condemned to Be Free," review of *Being and Nothingness,* by Jean-Paul Sartre, *New York Times Book Review,* 15 July 1956, 4; John Wild, "Living Philosophy," *Saturday Review* 6 (October 1956): 26.

59. Wild, "Living Philosophy," 26.

60. Barrett, "Condemned to Be Free," 4.

61. American Philosophical Association, *Proceedings of the Forty-Ninth Annual Meeting of the Western Division* (Yellow Springs, Ohio: American Philosophical Association, 1954), 40.

62. White, *The Age of Analysis,* 242; American Philosophical Association, *Proceedings of the Fifty-Third Annual Meeting of the Eastern Division* (Yellow Springs, Ohio: American Philosophical Association, 1958), 10.

63. Ibid., 16.

64. American Philosophical Association, *Proceedings of the Fifty-First Annual Meeting of the Eastern Division* (Yellow Springs, Ohio: American Philosophical Association, 1956), 16.

65. Ibid., 36.

66. Ibid., 36, 40.

67. Brand Blanshard, letter to author, 11 November 1979; Hazel Barnes, interview by author, tape recording, Boulder, Colo., 1979.

CHAPTER FIVE

1. Archie Bahm, ed., *The Directory of American Philosophers,* vol. 3 (Albuquerque: A. J. Bahm, 1967), 486–88.

2. Eugene Kaelin, letter to author, 24 October 1987.

3. Henri Peyre, letter to author, 10 August 1979; *Yale University Catalog, 1958–1959* (New Haven, Conn.: Yale University Press, 1958), 155.

4. *Harvard University Catalog, 1958–1959* (Cambridge, Mass.: Harvard University Press, 1958), 285.

5. Ibid., 280–82.

6. American Philosophical Association, *Proceedings of the Thirtieth Annual Meeting–Thirty-Sixth Annual Meeting of the Eastern, Western, and Pacific Divisions* (Yellow Springs, Ohio: American Philosophical Association, 1956–63).

7. Eugene Kaelin, letter to author, 24 October 1987.

8. Anna-Teresa Tymieniecka, "The History of American-Phenomenology-in Process," in *American Phenomenology: Origins and Developments,* ed. Eugene Kaelin and Calvin Schrag (Boston: Kluwer, 1989), xxi.

9. "Introductory Note," *Journal of Philosophy* 54 (May 1957): 313.

10. Gilbert Varet and Paul Kurtz, eds., *International Directory of Philosophy and Philosophers* (Atlantic Highlands, N.J.: Humanities, 1960), 190.

11. Jean-Paul Sartre, *The Transcendence of the Ego: An Existentialist Theory of Consciousness,* trans. Forrest Williams and Robert Kirkpatrick (New York: Noonday, 1957).

12. Forrest Williams, telephone conversation with author, 30 July 1990.

13. Jean-Paul Sartre, *Imagination: A Psychological Critique,* trans. Forrest Williams (Ann Arbor: University of Michigan Press, 1962).

14. William Barrett, *Irrational Man: A Study in Existential Philosophy* (Garden City, N.Y.: Doubleday, 1958); Robert Olson, *An Introduction to Existentialism* (New York: Dover, 1962); Marjorie Grene, *An Introduction to Existentialism* (Chicago: University of Chicago Press, 1959); Ralph Winn, ed., *A Concise Dictionary of Existentialism* (New York: Philosophical Library, 1960).

15. James Edie, "Transcendental Ontology and Existentialism," *Journal of Philosophy* 59 (October 1962): 681–84; John Wild, "Existentialism as a Philosophy," *Journal of Philosophy* 57 (January 1960): 45–62.

16. Herbert Spiegelberg, "Husserl's Phenomenology and Existentialism," *Journal of Philosophy* 58 (January 1960): 67.

17. Herbert Spiegelberg, *The Phenomenological Movement: An Historical Introduction* (The Hague: Nijhoff, 1960); William Earle, "Phenomenology and Existentialism," *Journal of Philosophy* (January 1960): 75–84; Maurice Natanson, "Phenomenology and Existentialism: Husserl and Sartre on Intentionality," *Modern Schoolman* 37 (November 1959): 1–10.

18. Spiegelberg, "Husserl's Phenomenology and Existentialism," 63, 64.

19. Ibid., 74.

20. Earle, "Phenomenology and Existentialism," 75, 76.

21. Ibid., 76, 83.

22. Natanson, "Phenomenology and Existentialism," 1–5.

23. Ibid., 5–10.

24. Barrett, *Irrational Man,* 297, 305.

25. Hans Meyerhoff, "The Return to the Concrete," *Chicago Review* 13 (Summer 1959): 27.

26. Tymieniecka, "The History of American Phenomenology-in-Process," xx.

27. William McBride, "John Wild and the Life-World," 99.

28. "Wild to Leave University for Post at Northwestern," *Harvard Crimson,* 11 May 1960, 2.

29. Ibid.

30. Paul Weiss, letter to author, 8 August 1990.

31. George Schrader, telephone conversation with author, 16 August 1990.

32. Barrett, *Irrational Man,* 18–19.

33. Meyerhoff, "The Return to the Concrete," 33; Hazel Barnes, "Existentialism in America" (lecture presented at the University of Colorado, Boulder, 28 July 1960).

34. Ibid.

35. Sidney Hook, "Pragmatism and Existentialism," *Antioch Review* 19 (Summer 1959): 153.

36. Barnes, "Existentialism in America"; Barrett, *Irrational Man,* 20.

37. Hook, "Pragmatism and Existentialism," 167.

38. Meyerhoff, "The Return to the Concrete," 27, 35.

39. Ibid., 30.

40. Ibid., 36.

41. Hazel Barnes, *The Literature of Possibility: A Study in Humanistic Existentialism* (Lincoln: University of Nebraska Press, 1959).

42. Rollo May, Ernest Angel, and Henri Ellenberger, eds., *Existence: A New Dimension in Psychiatry and Psychology* (New York: Basic, 1958); Meyerhoff, "The Return to the Concrete," 31.

43. May, Angel, and Ellenberger, eds., *Existence,* vii.

44. George Schrader, "Existential Psychoanalysis and Metaphysics," *Review of Metaphysics* 13 (September 1959): 162; Harry Tiebout, "Tillich, Existentialism and Psychoanalysis," *Journal of Philosophy* 56 (July 1959): 605–12.

45. Paul Kurtz, "Kierkegaard, Existentialism, and the Contemporary Scene," *Antioch Review* 21 (Spring 1961): 484.

46. Hook, "Pragmatism and Existentialism," 168.

47. Olson, *Introduction to Existentialism,* 13–29.

48. Alvin Plantinga, "An Existentialist's Ethics," *Review of Metaphysics* 12 (December 1958): 255.

49. Olson, *An Introduction to Existentialism,* 65; Kurtz, "Kierkegaard, Existentialism, and the Contemporary Scene," 484.

154 NOTES TO PAGES 118–29

50. Barrett, *Irrational Man*, 262.

51. Albert Levi, "The Quixotic Quest for Being," *Ethics* 66 (January 1956): 132–36, and "The Meaning of Existentialism for Contemporary International Relations," *Ethics* 72 (July 1962): 233–49.

52. Levi, "The Meaning of Existentialism," 249.

53. Jeff Mason, letter to author, 18 January 1989.

54. Olson, *An Introduction to Existentialism*, 64.

55. Bahm, ed., *The Directory of American Philosophers*, 488.

56. J. Glenn Gray, "Salvation on the Campus: Why Existentialism Is Capturing the Students," *Harper's Magazine*, May 1965, 53–60.

57. Ibid., 57.

58. Ibid., 54.

59. Ibid., 59.

60. Tymieniecka, "The History of American Phenomenology-in-Process," xxii.

61. William McBride, letter to author, 14 September 1989.

62. Jean-Paul Sartre, *Search for a Method*, trans. Hazel Barnes (New York: Knopf, 1963).

63. Ibid., viii.

64. Ibid., ix.

65. Hook, "Pragmatism and Existentialism," 151–68.

66. John Smith, *The Spirit of American Philosophy* (New York: Oxford University Press, 1963), 207–10.

67. Kurtz, "Kierkegaard, Existentialism, and the Contemporary Scene," 487.

68. James Tomberlin and Peter Van Inwagen, eds., *Alvin Plantinga* (Boston: D. Reidel, 1985), 9.

69. Barrett, *Irrational Man*, 3–8.

70. Smith, *The Spirit of American Philosophy*, viii.

71. Paul A. Schilpp, "The Abdication of Philosophy," in *Proceedings of the Fifty-Seventh Annual Meeting of the Eastern Division*, American Philosophical Association (Yellow Springs, Ohio: American Philosophical Association, 1962), 21.

72. John Randall, Jr., "Looking Is Better Than Just Talking," *Proceedings of the Fifty-First Annual Meeting of the Eastern Division*, American Philosophical Association (Yellow Springs, Ohio: American Philosophical Association, 1956), 18.

73. Hook, "Pragmatism and Existentialism," 168.

74. Kurtz, "Kierkegaard, Existentialism, and the Contemporary Scene," 487.

SELECTED BIBLIOGRAPHY

BOOKS

Anderson, Thomas. *The Foundation and Structure of Sartrean Ethics.* Lawrence, Kans.: Regents, 1974.

Bahm, Archie, ed. *The Directory of American Philosophers.* Vol. 3. Albuquerque: A. J. Bahm, 1967.

Barnes, Hazel. *The Literature of Possibility: A Study in Humanistic Existentialism.* Lincoln: University of Nebraska Press, 1959.

Barrett, William. *Irrational Man: A Study in Existential Philosophy.* Garden City, N.J.: Doubleday, 1958.

———. *What Is Existentialism?* 1947. Reprint, New York: Grove, 1964.

Baskin, Wade, ed. *Essays in Existentialism.* New York: Citadel, 1965.

Beauvoir, Simone de. *The Prime of Life.* Translated by Peter Green. New York: Harper, 1962.

———. *Force of Circumstance.* Translated by Richard Howard. New York: Putnam, 1964.

Binswanger, Ludwig. *Being-in-the-World: Selected Papers of Ludwig Binswanger.* Translated by Jacob Needleman. New York: Basic, 1953.

Blau, Joseph. *Men and Movements in American Philosophy.* New York: Prentice-Hall, 1952.

Boyer, Paul. *By the Bomb's Early Light: American Thought and Culture at the Dawn of the Atomic Age.* New York: Pantheon, 1985.

Cohen-Solal, Annie. *Sartre: A Life.* Translated by Anna Cancogni. New York: Pantheon, 1987.

Collins, James. *The Existentialists: A Critical Study.* Chicago: Henry Regnery, 1952.

Copleston, Frederic. *Friedrich Nietzsche: Philosopher of Culture.* London: Search Press, 1975.

Corsini, Raymond, ed. *Current Psychotherapies.* Itasca, Ill.: F. E. Peacock, 1975.

Del Vayo, J. Alvarez. "Politics and the Intellectual." *Nation,* 28 September 1946, 346–49.

Desan, Wilfrid. *The Tragic Finale: An Essay on the Philosophy of Jean-Paul Sartre.* Cambridge, Mass.: Harvard University Press, 1954.

———. *The Marxism of Jean-Paul Sartre.* New York: Doubleday, 1966.

Descombes, Vincent. *Modern French Philosophy.* Translated by L. Scott-Fox and J. M. Harding. London: Cambridge University Press, 1980.

Donagan, A., A. N. Perovich, Jr., and M. V. Weden, eds. *Human Nature and Natural Knowledge.* Dordrecht: D. Reidel, 1986.

Farber, Marvin, ed. *Philosophic Thought in France and the United States: Essays Representing Major Trends in French and American Philosophy.* Albany: State University of New York Press, 1950.

Flanner, Janet. *Paris Journal.* Vol. 1, *1944–1965.* New York: Atheneum, 1965.

Flynn, Thomas. *Sartre and Marxist Existentialism: The Test Case of Collective Responsibility.* Chicago: University of Chicago Press, 1984.

Grene, Marjorie. *Dreadful Freedom: A Critique of Existentialism.* Chicago: University of Chicago Press, 1948.

———. *An Introduction to Existentialism.* Chicago: University of Chicago Press, 1959.

———. *Philosophy In and Out of Europe.* Berkeley: University of California Press, 1976.

Grimsley, Ronald. *Existentialist Thought.* Cardiff: University of Wales Press, 1967.

Hanna, Thomas. *The Lyrical Existentialists.* New York: Atheneum, 1962.

Hannay, Alastair. *Kierkegaard.* London: Routledge and Kegan, 1982.

Hayman, Ronald. *Sartre: A Life.* New York: Simon and Schuster, 1987.

Heidegger, Martin. *Existence and Being.* Translated by Douglass Scott, R. F. C. Hull, and Alan Crick. Chicago: Henry Regnery, 1949.

Hook, Sidney. *Out of Step: An Unquiet Life in the Twentieth Century.* New York: Harper, 1987.

Hughes, H. Stuart. *The Obstructed Path: French Social Thought in the Years of Desperation, 1930–1960.* New York: Harper, 1968.

James, William. *The Varieties of Religious Experience: A Study in Human Nature.* New York: Modern Library, 1936.

Kaelin, Eugene, and Calvin Schrag, eds. *American Phenomenology: Origins and Developments.* Boston: Kluwer, 1989.

Kaufmann, Walter. *Existentialism from Dostoevsky to Sartre.* New York: Meridian, 1956.

Kern, Edith, ed. *Sartre: A Collection of Essays.* Englewood Cliffs, N.J.: Prentice-Hall, 1962.

Kuklick, Bruce. *The Rise of American Philosophy: Cambridge, Massachusetts, 1860–1930.* New Haven, Conn.: Yale University Press, 1977.

La Capra, Dominick. *A Preface to Sartre.* Ithaca, N.Y.: Cornell University Press, 1978.

Marx, Karl. *Early Writings.* Translated and edited by T. B. Bottomore. New York: McGraw-Hill, 1964.

May, Rollo, Ernest Angel, and Henri Ellenberger, eds. *Existence: A New Dimension in Psychiatry and Psychology.* New York: Basic, 1958.

Murdoch, Iris. *Sartre: Romantic Rationalist.* London: Bowes and Bowes, 1953.

Natanson, Maurice. *A Critique of Jean-Paul Sartre's Ontology.* Lincoln: University of Nebraska Press, 1951.

Olson, Robert. *An Introduction to Existentialism.* New York: Dover, 1962.

Peyre, Henri. *French Novelists of Today.* New York: Oxford University Press, 1967.

Pickles, Dorothy. *France between the Republics.* London: Love and Malcolmson, 1946.

Poster, Mark. *Existential Marxism in Postwar France: From Sartre to Althusser.* Princeton, N.J.: Princeton University Press, 1975.

Ranwez, Alain. *Jean-Paul Sartre's Les Temps Moderne: A Literary History, 1945–1962.* Troy, N.Y.: Whitson, 1981.

Reck, Andrew. *Recent American Philosophy: Studies of Ten Representative Thinkers.* New York: Pantheon, 1964.

Riesman, David, with Nathan Glazer and Reuel Denny. *The Lonely Crowd: A Study of the Changing American Character.* New Haven, Conn.: Yale University Press, 1950.

Rupp, George. *Beyond Existentialism and Zen: Religion in a Pluralistic World.* London: Oxford University Press, 1979.

Sartre, Jean-Paul. *Nausea.* Translated by Lloyd Alexander. Norfolk, Conn.: New Directions, n.d.

———. *L'Être et le néant: Essai d'ontologie phénoménologique.* Paris: Gallimard, 1943.

———. *The Age of Reason.* Translated by Eric Sutton. New York: Knopf, 1947.

———. *Existentialism.* Translated by Bernard Frechtman. New York: Philosophical Library, 1947.

———. *No Exit (Huis Clos): A Play in One Act and The Flies (Les Mouches): A Play in Three Acts.* Translated by Stuart Gilbert. New York: Knopf, 1947.

———. *The Reprieve.* Translated by Eric Sutton. New York: Knopf, 1947.

———. *The Emotions: Outline of a Theory.* Translated by Bernard Frechtman. New York: Philosophical Library, 1948.

———. *The Psychology of the Imagination.* Translated by Bernard Frechtman. New York: Philosophical Library, 1948.

———. *The War Diaries.* Translated by Quintin Hoare. New York: Philosophical Library, 1949.

———. *What Is Literature?* Translated by Bernard Frechtman. New York: Philosophical Library, 1949.

———. *Existential Psychoanalysis.* Translated by Hazel Barnes. Chicago: Henry Regnery, 1953.

———. *Being and Nothingness: A Phenomenological Essay on Ontology.* Translated by Hazel Barnes. New York: Washington Square, 1956.

———. *The Transcendence of the Ego: An Existentialist Theory of Consciousness.* Translated by Forrest Williams and Robert Kirkpatrick. New York: Noonday, 1957.

———. *Imagination: A Psychological Critique.* Translated by Forrest Williams. Ann Arbor: University of Michigan Press, 1962.

———. *Search for a Method.* Translated by Hazel Barnes. New York: Knopf, 1963.

———. *The Words.* Translated by Bernard Frechtman. New York: Braziller, 1964.

———. *Critique of Dialectical Reason: Theory of Practical Ensembles.* Translated by A. Sheridan-Smith. London: Humanities, 1976.

Schilpp, Paul, ed. *The Philosophy of Jean-Paul Sartre.* La Salle, Ill.: Open Court, 1981.

Spiegelberg, Herbert. *The Phenomenological Movement: A Historical Introduction.* Vol. 2. The Hague: Nijhoff, 1960.

Stern, Alfred. *Sartre: His Philosophy and Existential Psychoanalysis.* New York: Delacorte, 1953.

Tomberlin, James, and Peter Van Inwagen, eds. *Alvin Plantinga.* Boston: D. Reidel, 1985.

Varet, Gilbert, and Paul Kurtz, eds. *International Directory of Philosophy and Philosophers.* Atlantic Highlands, N.J.: Humanities Press, 1960.

White, Morton. *The Age of Analysis: Twentieth Century Philosophers*. Vol. 6, *The Great Ages of Western Philosophy*. Boston: Houghton-Mifflin, 1955.

Whyte, William. *The Organization Man*. New York: Simon and Schuster, 1956.

Wild, John. *The Challenge of Existentialism*. Bloomington: Indiana University Press, 1953.

Winn, Ralph, ed. *A Concise Dictionary of Existentialism*. New York: Philosophical Library, 1960.

Young-Bruehl, Elisabeth. *Freedom and Karl Jaspers's Philosophy*. New Haven, Conn.: Yale University Press, 1981.

Zabel, Morton, ed. *Literary Opinion in America*. New York: Harper, 1951.

ARTICLES

Ames, Van Meter. "Fetishism in the Existentialism of Sartre." *Journal of Philosophy* 47 (July 1950): 407–11.

———. "Reply to Mr. Natanson." *Journal of Philosophy* 48 (February 1951): 99–102.

———. "Existentialism and the Arts." *Journal of Aesthetics and Art Criticism* 8 (March 1951): 252–56.

Barres, Oliver. "In the Deeps of Despair." *Saturday Review of Literature*, 31 May 1947, 30.

Barrett, William. "The Talent and Career of Jean-Paul Sartre." *Partisan Review*, Spring 1946, 235–46.

———. "Condemned To Be Free." Review of *Being and Nothingness*, by Jean-Paul Sartre. *New York Times Book Review*, 15 July 1956.

Barzun, Jacques. "Ça Existe: A Note on the New Ism." *American Scholar*, October 1946, 449.

Beauvoir, Simone de. "Strictly Personal: Jean-Paul Sartre." Translated by Malcolm Cowley. *Harper's Bazaar*, January 1946, 113.

Blanshard, Brand. "From the Commissioner's Mailbag." *Philosophical Review* 54 (May 1945): 210–16.

Brown, John Lackey. "Chief Prophet of Existentialism." *New York Times Magazine*, 2 February 1947, 20.

Brown, Stuart. "The Atheistic Existentialism of Jean-Paul Sartre." *Philosophical Review* 57 (March 1948): 158–66.

Buchler, Justus. "Concerning *Existentialism*." *Nation*, October 1947, 449–50.

Burtt, Edwin. "What Happened in Philosophy from 1900 to 1950." *Allegheny College Bulletin* 7 (May 1952): 3–24.

Chiarmonte, Nicola. "Paris Letter: Sartre v. Camus, A Political Quarrel." *Partisan Review* 19 (November–December 1952), 680–86.

Coolidge, Mary. "Some Vicissitudes of the Once-Born and of the Twice-Born Man." *Philosophy and Phenomenological Research* 11 (September 1950): 75–87.

Earle, William. "Freedom and Existence: A Symposium." *Review of Metaphysics* 9 (September 1955): 46–56.

———. "Phenomenology and Existentialism." *Journal of Philosophy* 57 (January 1960): 75–84.

Edie, James. "Transcendental Ontology and Existentialism." *Journal of Philosophy* 59 (October 1962): 681–84.

"Existentialism." *Time,* 28 January 1946, 28.

Frizell, Bernard. "Existentialism: Postwar Paris Enthrones a Bleak Philosophy of Pessimism." *Life,* 7 June 1946, 59.

Gray, J. Glenn. "The Idea of Death in Existentialism." *Journal of Philosophy* 48 (March 1951): 113–27.

———. "Salvation on the Campus: Why Existentialism Is Capturing the Students." *Harper's Magazine,* May 1965, 53–60.

Grene, Marjorie. "L'Homme est une passion inutile: Sartre et Heidegger." *Kenyon Review* 9 (Spring 1947): 167–85.

———. "Sartre's Theory of the Emotions." *Yale French Studies* 1 (Spring–Summer 1948): 97–101.

Guerard, Albert. "French and American Pessimism." *Harper's Magazine,* September 1945, 276.

Hendel, Charles. "The Subjective as a Problem." *Philosophical Review* 62 (July 1953): 327–54.

Hook, Sidney. Review of *The Emotions,* by Jean-Paul Sartre. *New York Times,* 11 July 1948, 16.

———. "Symposium: Our Country and Our Culture." *Partisan Review* 19 (July–August 1952): 569–74.

———. "Pragmatism and Existentialism." *Antioch Review* 19 (Summer 1959): 151–68.

"Introductory Note." *Journal of Philosophy* 54 (May 1957): 313.

Kraushaar, Otto. Review of *A Kierkegaard Anthology,* by Robert Bretall, *Existentialism* by Jean-Paul Sartre, and "What is Existentialism?" by William Barrett. *Journal of Philosophy* 44 (December 1947): 715–21.

Kurtz, Paul. "Kierkegaard, Existentialism, and the Contemporary Scene." *Antioch Review* 21 (Spring 1961): 481–87.

Laguna, Grace de. "Speculative Philosophy." *Philosophical Review* 60 (January 1950): 155–76.

Levi, Albert. "The Quixotic Quest for Being." *Ethics* 66 (January 1956): 132–36.

———. "The Meaning of Existentialism for Contemporary International Research." *Ethics* 72 (July 1962): 233–44.

Marcuse, Herbert. "Remarks on Jean-Paul Sartre's *L'Être et le néant.*" *Philosophy and Phenomenological Research* 8 (March 1948): 311.

McGill, V. J. "Sartre's Doctrine of Freedom." *Revue Internationale de Philosophie* 9 (July 1949): 329–30.

Meyerhoff, Hans. "The Return to the Concrete." *Chicago Review* 13 (Summer 1959): 27–38.

Natanson, Maurice. "Sartre's Fetishism: A Reply to Van Meter Ames." *Journal of Philosophy* 48 (February 1951): 95–99.

———. "Jean-Paul Sartre's Philosophy of Freedom." *Social Research* 19 (September 1952): 364–80.

———. "Phenomenology and Existentialism: Husserl and Sartre on Intentionality." *Modern Schoolman* 37 (November 1959): 1–10.

Plantinga, Alvin. "An Existentialist's Ethics." *Review of Metaphysics* 12 (December 1958): 235–55.

"Pursuit of Wisdom: Existentialism, Lettrism and Sensorialism." *Time,* 2 December 1946, 20.

Randall, John. "Metaphysics: Its Function, Consequences and Criteria." *Journal of Philosophy* 43 (July 1946): 401–12.

——. "On Being Rejected." *Journal of Philosophy* 50 (December 1953): 797–805.

Rau, Catherine. "The Ethical Theory of Jean-Paul Sartre." *Journal of Philosophy* 46 (August 1949): 536–45.

——. "The Aesthetic Views of Jean-Paul Sartre." *Journal of Aesthetics and Art Criticism* 9 (Winter 1950): 137.

Rice, Philip. "Existentialism and the Self." *Kenyon Review* 12 (Spring 1950): 304–30.

Sartre, Jean-Paul. "Americans and Their Myths." *Nation,* 18 October 1947, 403.

Schrader, George. "Existence, Truth and Subjectivity." *Journal of Philosophy* 53 (November 1956): 759–71.

——. "Existential Psychoanalysis and Metaphysics." *Review of Metaphysics* 13 (September 1959): 139–69.

Sellars, Roy. "Review of *Existentialism,* by Jean-Paul Sartre." *American Sociological Review* 12 (October 1947): 725–26.

Smith, John. "Is Existence a Valid Philosophical Concept?" *Journal of Philosophy* 47 (April 1950): 238–49.

——. "The Revolt of Existence." *Yale Review* 43 (March 1954): 364–71.

Spiegelberg, Herbert. "French Existentialism: Its Social Philosophies." *Kenyon Review* 16 (Summer 1954): 448–54.

——. "Husserl's Phenomenology and Existentialism." *Journal of Philosophy* 58 (January 1960): 62–74.

Tiebout, Harry. "Existential Psychoanalysis and Metaphysics." *Journal of Philosophy* 54 (July 1959): 605–12.

Vayo, J. Alvarez del. "Politics and the Intellectual." *Nation,* 28 September 1946, 346–49.

PROCEEDINGS

American Philosophical Association. *Proceedings of the Fortieth–Fifty-Eighth Annual Meetings of the Eastern, Western and Central Divisions.* Yellow Springs, Ohio: American Philosophical Association, 1945–1963.

CATALOGS

Columbia University. *Catalog, 1948.* New York: Columbia University Press, 1947.

Harvard University. *Catalog, 1950.* Cambridge: Harvard University Press, 1949.

University of Chicago. *Catalog, 1948.* Chicago: Chicago University Press, 1947.

Yale University. *Catalog, 1958.* New Haven, Conn.: Yale University Press, 1957.

UNPUBLISHED MATERIALS

Barnes, Hazel. "Existentialism in America." Lecture presented at the University of Colorado, Boulder, 28 July 1960.

——. Letter to author, 11 June 1979.

——. Interview by author. Tape recording. Boulder, Colo., 1979.

——. Telephone conversation with author, 1 May 1979.

——. Telephone conversation with author, 12 November 1990.

Blanshard, Brand. Letter to author, 11 November 1979.

Brown, Stuart. Letter to author, 21 June 1990.

Cohn, Robert. Letter to author, 19 October 1979.

Cornish, Robert. Letter to author, 23 October 1979.

——. Letter to author, 13 October 1979.

——. Letter to author, 27 March 1989.

——. Letter to author, 13 October, 1989.

Cumming, Robert. Letter to author, 23 October 1979.

Danto, Arthur. Letter to author, 30 December 1989.

Desan, Wilfrid. Letter to author, 29 June 1990.

Duffy, Joan. Letter to author, 7 September 1988.

Fell, Joseph. Letter to author, 31 March 1980.

Greene, Maxine. Letter to author, 11 June 1979.

Grene, Marjorie. Letter to author, 6 December 1988.

Kaelin, Eugene. Letter to author, 9 July 1982.

——. Letter to author, 24 October 1987.

Mason, Jeff. Letter to author, 18 January 1989.

McBride, William. Letter to author, 14 September 1989.

Natanson, Maurice. Letter to author, 4 July 1990.

——. Telephone conversation with author, 1 April 1989.

Newhall, David. Interview by author. Portland, 20 May 1979.

——. Telephone conversation with author, 31 October 1990.

Peyre, Henri. Letter to author, 10 August 1979.

Quine, Willard. Letter to author, 10 September 1979.

Randall, Francis. Letter to author, 24 November 1979.

Rau, Catherine. Telephone conversation with author, 21 April 1989.

Schiff, Judith. Letter to author, 21 November 1988.

Schrader, George. Telephone conversation with author, 16 August 1990.

Smith, John. Letter to author, 6 March 1989.

Weiss, Paul. Letter to author, 8 August 1990.

Williams, Forrest. Telephone conversation with author, 30 July 1990.

INDEX

Absurdism, 95, 108

Algeria, French colonialism in, 9

America: aesthetic theory in, 54,
56, 125; anticommunism in, 16,
45, 88; European thought shared
by, *see* Continental thought;
existentialism/Sartreanism in, 1–5,
19, 107–9, 139, (debate over) 68–73,
(evolution of) 4, 49, 58, 62, 112,
135–36, (four stages of response:
initial, second, consideration of
paradoxes, final) 20–47, 48–82, 83–
110, 111–42, (and freedom) 9–10,
74, (hostility or indifference
toward) 28–40, 43–47, 54–56, 63,
71, 78, 80, 92, 109, (key issue,
1950s) 83–85, 101, (language
barrier) 25–27, 37, 44–45, 49, 50,
85, 111, 115, 136, (similarity to
American thought) 56–57,
(university courses) 21–23, 33, 43,
49–53, 76–78, 97, 111–13, 121–22,
131–33; male predominance in
philosophical field, 3, 79, 142;
Sartre's views of policies of, 9, 31–
32, 67–68, 82, 90; Sartre visits, 25,
31; in World War II, 21, 31, 32, 34.
See also Anglo-American thought

American Philosophical Association,
58; papers presented at meetings,
59, 63; presidential addresses, 81,
88, 91, 106–8, 139, 140; symposia of,
95, 105, 111–12, 113–14, 117

American Scholar magazine, 28

American Society for Aesthetics, 54

Ames, Van Meter, 55–56, 94, 138;
Natanson debate, 68–72

Analytic philosophy, 34, 38–39, 50–51,
59, 92, 95–96; Continental thought
and, 96, 106–8, 120–21; criticized,
46, 85, 93, 94, 136–37, 140–41

Angel, Ernest, 126

Anglo-American thought, 7, 95;
Continental thought and, 3, 7, 16,
45, 51, 95 (*see also* Continental
thought); and existentialism, 60,
62–63, 72, 81, 103–7 *passim;* Sartre
disavows, 85. *See also* Analytic
philosophy

Antioch Review, 127

Aristotelian thought, 66

Atheism, 5, 61, 109, 138

Atlantic Charter, 67, 68

Authenticity, concept of, 73, 74–76, 87

Ayer, Alfred, 109

Bahm, Archie, 131

Barnes, Hazel, 63, 76–80 *passim,* 113,
115, 123; translates Sartre, 2, 26, 83–
84, 102–4, 109–12 *passim,* 116, 133,
134, 138; *The Literature of
Possibility,* 125, 137

Barres, Oliver, 29, 33

Barrett, William, 71, 123–24; defends
Sartreanism, 21, 35–43 *passim,* 104,
105, 113; and Sartrean politics, 56,
67, 68, 82, 129; *Irrational Man,* 35,
43, 116, 120, 122

Barzun, Jacques, 28–29

Beat movement, 131

Beauvoir, Simone de, 6–7, 11, 12, 17

Being and nonbeing, discussion of,
100–1

Berger, Gaston, 113

Bergson, Henri, 6

Binswanger, Ludwig: *Daseinanalyse,*
86

Blanshard, Brand, 89, 109, 122

Bretall, Robert, 43

Brown, John Lackey, 29, 30–32, 33

Brown, Stuart, 21, 66, 74

Buchler, Justus, 35–38 *passim,* 40, 42, 44

Burch, George, 121

Burtt, Edwin, 39

Camus, Albert, 109; *L'Homme révolté*, 89
Capitalism, Sartre's view of, 7, 46
Carnap, Rudolf, 41, 53, 106
Catholic thought, 12, 18; and anti-Catholicism, 6; and existentialism, 2
Chiarmonte, Nicola, 89
Chicago Review, 120
Christianity, 5, 103
Cohn, Robert, 21, 22–23
Cold War, 9, 34, 45, 46, 68, 81
Columbia University, 76, 96, 112
Communism and Communist Party: and anticommunism, 16, 45, 88; French, 8, 18, 88–89; Sartre and, 8–9, 65–68 *passim*, 82, 88–91, 109, 129; Sartreanism as viewed by, 8, 12, 15–16
Concreteness, standard of, 16–17
Consciousness, theory of, 4–5, 7–8, 9, 52, 54, 93, 97, 115
Continental thought, 3, 7, 20, 34, 37, 45, 72; American philosophy and, 16, 84, 94–95, 106–8; American scholarship shares, 49–51, 58–62, 85, 97, 112–15, 120–21, 139, 141; German existentialism, 24, 53, 55, 74, 79, 131. *See also* France
Coolidge, Mary, 60–62, 79
Cornish, Robert, 26–27
Cumming, Robert, 21, 26, 113, 114

Danto, Arthur, 50–51, 115
Del Vayo, J. Alvarez, 29–30
Depression, the, 79
Desan, Wilfred, 99, 113; *The Tragic Finale*, 87, 98
Descartes, René, and Cartesian thought, 6, 7, 9, 13, 22, 24, 77, 137
Dewey, John, 57, 123
Dilthey, Wilhelm, 70
Directory of American Philosophers, The (Bahm, ed.), 131
Dos Passos, John, 23
Douglas, Kenneth, 22–23, 24

Earle, William, 98–99, 113, 115, 117, 118–19
Edie, James, 133
Eisenhower, General Dwight, 88
Ellenberger, Henri, 126
Emerson, Ralph Waldo, 57
Empiricism, 54; radical, of James, 3, 136; Sartre's rejection of, 52–56 *passim*, 63, 68–70, 82
Ethical issues, 2, 39–40, 64, 127–30, 139
Ethics (periodical), 129
Europe. *See* Continental thought
Existence: A New Dimension in Psychiatry and Psychology (May, Angel, Ellenberger, eds.), 125–26
Existentialism: "American," 107–9, 139 (*see also* America); *Concise Dictionary of,* 116; defined, 4–5, 43; French and German, *see* Continental thought; industrialization as viewed by, 5–6; Marxism and, *see* Marxism; and metaphysics, 40, 41, 69, 71; modern, Kierkegaard and, 5; phenomenological vs. traditional, 117 (*see also* Phenomenology); realism and, 93, 95; Sartre's early, 1, 6; and science, 94; student interest/instruction in, 4, 33, 43, 141, (World War II and postwar) 21–23, 49–52, (1950s, early 1960s) 30, 76–78, 97, 111–13, 121–22, 130–33. *See also* Sartreanism
Existentialism from Dostoevsky to Sartre (Kaufmann, ed.), 84–85, 112
Existential psychoanalysis. *See* Psychoanalysis

Farber, Marvin, 51
Faulkner, William, 23
Fell, Joseph, 27, 77, 78
Figaro (French newspaper), 31
Flanner, Janet, 11–12, 15
Ford, Charles Henri, 25
France, 6, 9, 54, 84; American

authors attracted to, 23, 26; Communist Party in, 8, 18, 88–89; existentialism/Sartreanism in, 1–4, 17, 34, 38, 44, 105, 108, (as fad) 11, 30, 36, 52, (postwar) 8, 11–16, 18–27 *passim,* 84, (vs. American approach) 72, 73, 75; and French Resistance (World War II), 12, 14, 15, 28, 63, 64–65, 90; liberation of Paris, 1, 15; philosophic views shared by Americans, 16, 51, 58, 60, 61, 62, 81

Frechtman, Bernard, 26

Freedom: centrality of concept, 9–10, 40, 41–42, 66–74 *passim,* 82, 86–87, 90, 97–100, 128; World War II and, 34, 69

Freud, Sigmund, 86, 126–27

Frizell, Bernard, 29, 30, 31, 33

Fulbright fellowships, 22, 50, 51, 69, 115, 123

German thought. *See* Continental thought

Gray, J. Glenn, 75, 131–33

Greene, Maxine, 78, 79

Grene, Marjorie, 39, 40, 45, 53–54, 62–66 *passim,* 74, 75, 79–80; *Dreadful Freedom,* 36–37, 57, 80, 116

Guicharnaud, Jacques, 13–14

Gurwitsch, Aron, 133

Harper's, 29, 131

Harper's Bazaar, 36

Harvard Crimson (undergraduate newspaper), 121

Harvard University, 77, 96, 112, 113, 121–22

Havet, Jacques, 16

Hegel, Georg, 5, 9, 45, 70, 77, 89, 112; Hegelian idealism, 5, 19, 57; neo- and post-Hegelianism, 24, 34, 101; Sartre's indebtedness to, 10–11, 17, 101, 105, 113

Heidegger, Martin, 37, 45, 70, 74, 79,

100, 126; Sartre influenced by/ compared to, 9, 10–11, 24, 53, 86, 113; *Existence and Being,* 51

Hemingway, Ernest, 23

Hendel, Charles, 93–95, 96, 100, 101, 105, 120, 122

Herodotus: *History,* 140

Hitler, Adolf, 7

Hook, Sidney, 57, 100–1, 114, 127; opposes Sartre, 49, 55, 67–68, 82, 89–90, 91, 124, 139, 141

Hume, David, 95

Hungarian revolt (1956), 8–9, 88

Husserl, Edmund, 7, 9–10, 17, 45, 51, 70, 71, 121; Husserlian phenomenology, 10, 117–18, 119

Idealism, 77; "alimentary philosophies" of, 7; Hegelian, 5, 57

Individualism, 24, 29, 40, 64, 70; Americans and, 34, 41, 75, 82, 140

Industrialization as threat, 5–6

International Day of Resistance against War and Fascism (1949), 67

James, William, 3, 61, 62, 122–23, 136, 140; *The Varieties of Religious Experience,* 103

Jaspers, Karl, 23, 45, 74, 79, 86, 126

Journal of Aesthetics and Art Criticism, 54, 55, 56

Journal of Philosophy, 43, 57, 68, 70, 94, 95, 100, 105, 114, 115, 125, 126

Kaelin, Eugene, 51, 112, 113

Kant, Immanuel, 6, 64, 112, 120

Kaufmann, Walter, 84–85, 89, 92, 112

Kenyon College, 60, 72, 97

Kenyon Review, 37, 60, 90

Kierkegaard, Søren, 5, 9, 38, 43, 70, 117–20 *passim,* 127

Kirkpatrick, Robert, 115

Kraushaar, Otto, 25, 37–38, 40–44 *passim,* 63

Kurtz, Paul, 127, 129, 130, 137–38, 142